Cambridge Elements ≡

Elements in Shakespeare and Pedagogy
edited by
Liam E. Semler
University of Sydney
Gillian Woods
Birkbeck College, University of London

TEACHING SHAKESPEARE AND HIS SISTERS

An Embodied Approach

Emma Whipday
Newcastle University

CAMBRIDGE
UNIVERSITY PRESS

CAMBRIDGE
UNIVERSITY PRESS

Shaftesbury Road, Cambridge CB2 8EA, United Kingdom

One Liberty Plaza, 20th Floor, New York, NY 10006, USA

477 Williamstown Road, Port Melbourne, VIC 3207, Australia

314–321, 3rd Floor, Plot 3, Splendor Forum, Jasola District Centre, New Delhi – 110025, India

103 Penang Road, #05–06/07, Visioncrest Commercial, Singapore 238467

Cambridge University Press is part of Cambridge University Press & Assessment, a department of the University of Cambridge.

We share the University's mission to contribute to society through the pursuit of education, learning and research at the highest international levels of excellence.

www.cambridge.org
Information on this title: www.cambridge.org/9781108972161

DOI: 10.1017/9781108975650

First published 2023

A catalogue record for this publication is available from the British Library.

ISBN 978-1-108-97216-1 Paperback
ISSN 2632-816X (online)
ISSN 2632-8151 (print)

Additional resources for this publication at www.cambridge.org/whipday.

Teaching Shakespeare and His Sisters

An Embodied Approach

Elements in Shakespeare and Pedagogy

DOI: 10.1017/9781108975650
First published online: June 2023

Emma Whipday
Newcastle University

Author for correspondence: Emma Whipday, emma.whipday@ncl.ac.uk

ABSTRACT: What are we teaching, when we teach Shakespeare? Today, the Shakespeare classroom is often also a rehearsal room; we teach Shakespeare plays as both literary texts and cues for theatrical performance. This Element explores the possibilities of an 'embodied' pedagogical approach as a tool to inform literary analysis. The first section offers an overview of the embodied approach, and how it might be applied to Shakespeare plays in a playhouse context. The second applies this framework to the play-making, performance, and storytelling of early modern women – 'Shakespeare's sisters' – as a form of feminist historical recovery. The third suggests how an embodied pedagogy might be possible digitally, in relation to online teaching. In so doing, this Element makes the case for an embodied pedagogy for teaching Shakespeare.

KEYWORDS: Shakespeare, embodied, performance, pedagogy, women writers

ISBNs: 9781108972161 (PB), 9781108975650 (OC)
ISSNs: 2632-816X (online), 2632-8151 (print)

Contents

This Element also has Online Appendices, available at www.cambridge.org/whipday. Appendices 1, 2, and 3 contain the extracts used in Section 2, with modernised spelling. Extract 3 of Appendix 3 is co-edited with Ruth Connolly. Appendix 4 contains stable links to two productions discussed in Section 2.

Introduction

What are we teaching, when we teach Shakespeare? Today, the Shakespeare classroom is often also a rehearsal room, which encourages students to 'minimize the distinction' between literary and theatrical ways of approaching these plays (Bevington, 2016, p. 44). We therefore teach Shakespeare plays as both literary texts and cues for theatrical performance. Much of this approach has been pioneered by the education departments of theatres and cultural institutions closely identified with the works of Shakespeare, often with a school-centred focus on a 'rehearsal room pedagogy' that involves putting Shakespeare 'on its feet' (Winston, 2015, pp. 53–74) and in 'students' mouths' (Folger Shakespeare Library, 'The Folger Method'). As Fiona Banks writes,

> Reading his plays without any form of active engagement,
> without his words in our mouths and emotions and actions
> in our bodies, is like trying to engage with a piece of music
> by looking at the notes on the page but not listening to the
> music itself... (2013, p. 3)[1]

Each of these approaches – to 'feet', 'mouths' and 'bodies '– takes embodiment as the central framework through which the works of Shakespeare can be taught. Rex Gibson, in his influential *Teaching Shakespeare*, likewise suggests that 'a Shakespeare script is a blueprint', and that 'active learning' is necessary to enable students to engage with Shakespeare's 'plays as plays' (1998, p. vi). These authors argue that Shakespeare's plays are written for embodied performance, and therefore reading these plays with and through bodies and voices enables an understanding of the plays that isn't accessible via silent reading or text-based study.

An emphasis on Shakespeare's plays as best understood in performance is also increasingly common in English Literature university classrooms, although a focus on what Milla Cozart Riggio calls the 'theatrical values' of Shakespeare's plays (1999, pp. 3–4) is still more likely to be theoretical than practical. Neil Thew's 2006 survey of fifty-one higher education institutions

---

[1] See also Cohen, 2018, which offers the motto 'always perform'.

in Britain revealed that 'performance activities are relatively little used [in the teaching of Shakespeare] at present' (p. 18); as Edward Rocklin argued in 2005, teaching Shakespeare through performance involves 'reframing' the 'practices traditionally employed in the literary study of drama' (p. xvi). Nearly two decades later, my own experiences (and those of colleagues) have suggested that some students (and, indeed, teachers) of English Literature at university level may be wary of the reframing and disciplinary boundary-crossing involved in participating in drama exercises in the literature classroom.[2]

Teaching Shakespeare and His Sisters: An Embodied Approach argues for such reframing and boundary-crossing. This Element explores the possibilities of active, embodied learning as a tool to inform literary analysis; such an approach does not 'minimise' the distinction between the literary and the theatrical, but, rather, demonstrates how an informed theatrical approach to a Shakespearean playtext can open up possibilities for literary analysis. An 'embodied' approach involves invoking the senses (particularly sight, hearing, and our 'sixth' sense, proprioception – the sense of the body in space), and inviting students to engage with playtexts as situated in (and shaped by) the time, space, and structures of performance.[3] *Teaching Shakespeare and His Sisters* offers a range of practical pedagogical activities to demonstrate how such an approach can provide a kinaesthetic way of unpacking the language, staging, and ideology of Shakespeare's plays – and those of his 'sisters'. In so doing, this Element suggests that teaching through performance and embodiment can do more than draw attention to the theatrical context of the playhouse; it can also offer an opportunity to engage with the wider performance contexts of early modern England – contexts in which women, as well as men, participate in play-making.

[2] I am grateful to my Literature and Drama colleagues at Eleanor Rycroft's University of Bristol event on Early Modern Digital Practice, 16 December 2020, for discussing the differing disciplinary expectations brought by students (and teachers).

[3] See Swale, 2015, p. xvi. On the benefits of an embodied approach to learning, see for example Wagner Cook, Mitchell, and Goldin-Meadow, 2008; and Abrahamson and Sánchez-García, 2016, pp. 203–39.

There are political and pedagogical reasons for teaching Shakespeare in the context of the theatre-making of his sisters: as an act of feminist historical recovery that seeks to introduce students to marginalised voices from the past, and to animate these voices through embodied reading. Ayanna Thompson and Laura Turchi note that one twenty-first-century habit of learning is the 'explicit exploration of identity' (2016, pp. 5, 1): teaching Shakespeare alongside his sisters enables students to explore the questions of identity that 'preoccupy' our twenty-first-century students, while offering a more complex, more nuanced, and more informed understanding of both early modern theatrical culture, and women's experiences in early modern England. Over the past fifty years of teaching Shakespeare, feminist perspectives have, as Phyllis Rackin puts it, 'transformed how we teach Shakespeare's plays' in relation to 'evidence of life experiences of women in Shakespeare's England' (2016, p. 10). Yet students are still likely to bring to the classroom certain assumptions about the 'oppressed' nature of women in the period, and about how Shakespeare's engagement with this is shaped by the 'all-male' early modern stage (a version of theatre history that has been challenged by recent research).[4]

Indeed, in his survey of UK university English teachers, Thew noted that '[t]he great majority of respondents discussed their sense of needing to help students examine and challenge their prior assumptions about Shakespeare; [and] his literary and historical contexts' (2006, p. 6).[5] These prior assumptions can be a Shakespeare teacher's greatest challenge; Derval Conroy and Danielle Clarke note that 'the sense of familiarity engendered by the presence of the Renaissance in popular culture' can be an 'obstacle' to student 'engagement with the specificities of a particular historical moment' (2011, p. 1).[6] The prevailing assumptions about early modern performance culture are, I find,

---

[4] Rackin, 2016, p. 10. See Korda, 2011; A Bit Lit, 2021; and the work of Cockett et al, n.d.

[5] I am grateful to the school teachers and academics at the RSA Conference on Innovative Online Teaching, 30 June 2021, for sharing their own experiences of this, and enabling me to reflect on mine.

[6] Conroy and Clarke focus on teaching in the UK, the United States, Europe, and Australia. On the political implications of failing to defamiliarise the past, see Eklund and Hyman, 2019, p. 7.

encapsulated by the 1998 film *Shakespeare in Love* (though today's students are
unlikely to have been born when that film was released). The only women
who exist in Tom Stoppard and Mark Norman's vision of the theatrical world
are: the nameless prostitutes who are moved spectators of *Romeo and Juliet*;
a lusty seamstress who is passed around between the men of the company;
Elizabeth I, who becomes Shakespeare's patron; and Viola de Lesseps, who
cross-dresses as a boy in order to act in Shakespeare's play, but must then
return to her elite world. Women, and their talents, exist only as sexual
objects, or to enable or appreciate men's genius; it is the men who, ultimately,
are the theatre. This is the narrative that many students will bring to the
classroom. Exploring wider possibilities for female agency, creativity, and
performance can offer students the opportunity to engage with questions of
identity, to challenge the marginalisation of female voices in the past, and to
attain a more nuanced understanding of how Shakespeare's plays engage with
gendered experiences in early modern England.

An embodied approach to teaching Shakespeare, then, not only enables
students to explore Shakespeare's theatrical potential by reading his plays as
plays, but offers three further pedagogical benefits:

(1) In close reading: embodied activities are tools that can help students
to close read literary and dramaturgical elements of early modern
plays, from direct address and stage directions to gendered power
dynamics.
(2) In reading Shakespeare's plays in relation to theatre history: an understanding of early modern cultures of performance (in and beyond the
professional playhouse) can enable students to comprehend how these
cultures shaped Shakespeare's playtexts.
(3) In accessing and analysing women's theatre-making: theatrical tools more
commonly used to analyse plays for the professional stage can be applied
to female-authored plays, female performances, and 'lost' female voices.

This Element demonstrates how an embodied, performance-based, active
approach can assist students in developing insights about a historicised
Shakespeare, situated within early modern cultural and performance contexts.
In so doing, it provides practical instructions for incorporating this approach
into the English Literature classroom.

Teaching Shakespeare and His Sisters offers examples of, and reflections on, pedagogical strategies that are equally applicable to school students preparing for university, and to undergraduate English Literature students. The activities in this Element can also be, and have been, used in primary education, postgraduate education, rehearsal in a theatrical context, and teaching in a heritage context, but this Element does not focus on these contexts. Rather, its emphasis is on approaches to Shakespeare for students of English Literature, seeking to develop advanced skills in literary analysis and in a historically-informed understanding of Shakespeare. Such skills form the focus of many Shakespeare classrooms and seminar rooms at A-Level (in the UK), Advanced Placement (in the United States), or International Baccalaureate, as well as in undergraduate courses internationally. While many of these activities may be of use to Drama teachers, the emphasis here is not only on how these activities and approaches may facilitate a theatrical understanding of Shakespeare's plays, but also upon how they enable a literary, feminist, and historical understanding of Shakespeare's plays (and of early modern English culture more broadly). While some of these activities involve a form of reflective writing (Activity 1) or creative writing (Activity 7) less common to the Literature classroom, all of the activities in this Element are designed to facilitate the kinds of literary skills – close reading, the use of supporting textual evidence, engagement with pertinent historical and theatrical contexts – assessed by traditional forms of literature assessment, such as the essay.[7] They are not designed to function as a replacement of or alternative to literary analysis, but rather, to inform such analysis.

The teaching in this Element is 'research-led', in that it shares materials from my own research; I therefore signpost my research (as well as that of others), and point the reader towards the practice-as-research experiments that have informed the development of these activities.[8] It is also 'research-oriented'

[7] These activities can also prepare students for more creative forms of assessment; Thompson and Turchi offer a rich range of creative assessment possibilities (2016).

[8] On 'research-led' teaching, see Healey, 2005, pp. 67–78. On 'practice-as-research', see for example Purcell, 2017. I am grateful to James Harriman-Smith for his insights when teaching our co-taught MA module 'Thinking Through Performance'.

(Healey, 2005), in that it enables students to experiment with the methodologies offered by the teacher. Practice-as-research in the study of Shakespeare and early modern drama can offer what have been described as 'fleeting encounters with the past' (Dustagheer, Jones, and Rycroft, 2017, p. 173) as part of 'a living process where theatre is experienced as having a vibrant existence beyond texts' (Cave, 2003, p. 11).[9] Engaging students in practice-as-research offers them the opportunity to experience the theatrical vibrancy of these historicised encounters. Furthermore, as Rocklin argues, a performance-framed teaching model calls attention to theatre as an ensemble practice, and to 'the ways in which the players and playgoers must function as co-creators of the performance' with the playwright (Rocklin, 2005, p. 73). This Element explores how students can themselves become 'co-creators' of the insights and analysis produced through these activities, offering the students the opportunity to become a source of authority in the classroom, as Section 1 further explores.

This Element is personal, drawn from my own research and teaching experiences, but it is also informed by pedagogical literature (both general and subject-specific) and by conversations with university and secondary-school teachers, both formal and informal. The activities in this Element are not my own – or rather, not uniquely my own. Teaching is collaborative, and many of these activities were developed with colleagues, created within the context of co-taught or team-taught modules, or inspired by the ideas of others. I am grateful to the colleagues in a range of teaching and performance contexts across universities, schools, and rehearsal rooms, whose expertise and generosity have shaped my teaching in general and these activities in particular.[10] Jessica Swale notes that no collection of drama games is original: 'games, like the plots of plays, are continually shared,

---

[9] See also Cox Jensen and Whipday, 2017.

[10] My debts of gratitude are too many to enumerate here, and many are specified in relation to particular activities below. I am particularly grateful to colleagues and collaborators at Shakespeare's Globe and the American Shakespeare Center; to my teachers and colleagues at Oxford, UCL, King's College London, and Newcastle University, with especial thanks to Helen Hackett; to Gill Woods, for her inspiring work in running Shakespeare Teachers' Conversation; and to both Gill and Liam E. Semler for their transformative feedback on this Element.

borrowed, adapted and recycled' (2015, p. x) – and this is equally true of these activities. The embodied approach itself was inspired by my own experience of learning from actor and theatre-maker Philip Bird, whose playful, enactive teaching methods inform many of these activities. And the most significant influence of all is that of my students: their engagement in shaping these activities has been integral (and some of their insights are quoted in Section 3 and the Conclusion).

Teaching Shakespeare and His Sisters offers a practical toolkit for school and university teachers seeking to incorporate creative, embodied, performance-based activities in the teaching of Shakespeare. This Element contains nine activities across three sections. Section 1 focuses upon teaching Shakespeare and embodiment through a playhouse context; Section 2 explores embodied ways of teaching female play-making and performance; and Section 3 reflects upon the possibilities for teaching Shakespeare through embodiment online, in the context of the shift to online teaching during the Covid-19 pandemic. To make the less familiar historical materials in Section 2 more accessible, explanations of the genres (masques, closet dramas, and witch trial accounts) are provided, and modern spelling extracts are available in the online appendices. Each activity in Sections 1 and 2 offers an optional follow-up activity; in Section 1, this offers a way to further develop the skills acquired in undertaking the original activity, while in Section 2, this offers a way to use the previous activity to explore a female-authored text. The activities in Section 3 are less specific, and therefore more broadly applicable; they can be applied to any early modern play.

The embodied activities in this Element are designed to develop a mode of reading: a way of paying attention to bodies in texts, and to plays as embodied texts. All the activities in this Element can be adjusted to accommodate disabled students for whom the requirement of movement through space might be a barrier to participation; in cases where this is not self-evident, I suggest ways it can be done. All activities are open to students using mobility aids. The activities in this Element aim to foster a playful, supportive, inclusive learning environment; this kind of embodied learning can be particularly helpful for students who prefer a kinaesthetic learning style, or for whom sustained text-based work and quiet classroom conditions can inhibit learning (see Whitfield, 2020). For students unable or unwilling to participate in the activities in Sections 1 and 2, Section 3 explores the ways in which an embodied approach can be facilitated digitally; the activities offered in this section can also be incorporated into a text-based classroom approach.

The most significant barrier to incorporating embodied activities in the classroom can be student discomfort, particularly among students who, in choosing a literature module, did not expect to learn through their bodies. The activities in this Element are designed to alleviate this discomfort through creating a participatory community in which students can work together, rather than a theatrical environment in which students might feel they are required to perform and be judged. These activities are designed to be performed by students simultaneously, so that there is no sense of some students being 'on display' to others; while many activities involve possibilities for students to volunteer to perform before the group, this is never a requirement, and in small group work, there are both 'actor' and 'director' roles available.

Active approaches to early modern performance, as Miranda Fay Thomas has observed of teaching with 'cue-scripts', offer students a way to embrace mistakes and the possibility for failure, and to 'liberate themselves from modern ideas of theatrical "perfection"' (2019, p. 128). Early modern playing conditions – including extremely limited rehearsal and a visible, audible, judging audience – required a playful, improvisatory, risky approach to the possibilities for failure, within a sociable performance context. Creating a supportive, playful learning environment that mimics the risk-taking, pleasure-seeking environments of early modern playhouses – where there is no expectation of rehearsed, polished performances, where all students are equally involved in experimenting together, where 'play' is emphasised, and where community is developed – can go a long way towards mitigating student anxiety, and building embodied confidence in the classroom. Inviting the students to imagine themselves as 'stepping back in time' can frame such activities in a playful way, while explaining how each activity develops historical awareness and skills in literary analysis can demonstrate the value of this approach.

This is not to suggest that discomfort can be avoided altogether; rather, that working through discomfort around embodied learning in a supportive environment can offer students (and teachers) both pedagogical and personal benefits. Student reflections on a third-year research-led module I co-designed and co-taught with Kate Chedgzoy, 'Gender, Power, and Performance in Early Modern Culture', suggest that discomfort need not be a barrier to participation. On this module, students were introduced to embodied learning in the first seminar, when they were invited (though not required) to participate in the first activity offered by this Element (Activity 1). This activity asks students to imaginatively 'embody' early modern men and women (of varying statuses), and then to reflect on their own embodied experience of intersecting identities, and how this shapes their experience of historicised embodiment. Further performance-based activities were incorporated into subsequent seminars. In an assessed reflective portfolio at the end of the module, many students noted that while they were 'initially apprehensive' about participating in Activity 1, they found embodied learning in practice was 'less daunting than [they] anticipated', and 'gain[ed] confidence' through participation. One student offered a particularly insightful reflection:

> I can remember my horror when we were asked to stand in the first seminar and enact the strides of different theatre-goers ... returning to our seats, my anxiety changed to determination – I wanted to enjoy participating in performance activities without feeling overwhelmed with discomfort when taking up space ... Throughout this process of growth, I have gained a better understanding of staging relevant to Early Modern theatre, as well as a palpable increase in confidence that I will take through life.

Some students may feel apprehensive or daunted, or even (as in this case) horrified, at the possibility of participating in any kind of embodied learning in the literature classroom. This student frames her anxiety about embodied participation in relation to her expectations of a seated, text-based classroom (Monk et al., as proponents of 'Open-Space Learning', might describe this

as learning 'with chairs' [2011, p. 6]); her 'horror' and 'anxiety' is invoked
by being 'asked to stand', to leave the familiarity of learning in her seat. As
this example demonstrates, leaning into this discomfort can enable students
to gain both a 'better understanding' of early modern theatre and increased
confidence in (and beyond) the classroom. This student went on to say:

> As a working-class woman, I have sometimes struggled to find
> confidence in academic settings . . . I have learned that I deserve
> to and should take up space (verbal and physical) . . . Active
> and unabashed participation is empowering[.][11]

For this student, paying embodied attention to historicised power
dynamics enabled her to reflect on – and to transform – her experience
of these dynamics today, 'tak[ing] up space' with both her body and her
voice. The activities in this Element offer students the opportunity to
'take up space' in the Shakespeare classroom – and, by extension, in the
academy, and even in the world beyond. 'Active and unabashed participation' in such activities can be confidence-building, 'empowering', and
offer a way to reflect on (and even to mitigate) the societal inequalities
that are likely to be present in the spatial and vocal politics of our
teaching institutions.

The activities in this Element can be used independently, or in any order,
with one exception: Activity 1, with which I suggest all teachers begin.
Sonya Freeman Loftis argues that 'Shakespeare criticism . . . often conveys
a sense of the author as a disengaged and disembodied critic who reads the
works of Shakespeare from an imagined impersonal viewpoint' (2021, p. 2):
inviting students to reflect on their own intersecting identities, and indeed,
reflecting on our own identities as teachers, can be a first step towards a form
of 'engaged and embodied' criticism, interrogating how these texts

---

[11] I am grateful to all the students on the module for their active and engaged
participation in difficult circumstances, and I am particularly grateful to those
who generously permitted me to share their reflections here. I am also grateful to
Kate Chedgzoy, with whom many of these seminars were co-taught, and whose
teaching on this module has influenced – and inspired – my own.

represent and replicate power structures and assumptions (gendered, racialised, class-based) about bodily norms. What is key is that, as Thompson and Turchi argue,

> There should be no *neutral* bodies in a classroom that embraces a theatre-based or kinaesthetic approach ... Students not only bring their modern bodies and modern interpretations of them, but also interrogate what it takes and means to perform in/as them. (2016, p. 84)

The kind of reflective interrogation that this activity offers can help to make 'normative' bodies on the early modern stage (and in early modern society) as visible to students as non-normative bodies, and encourage students to consider the power structures that shape how identity is performed. Students are usually accustomed to the fact that boy players played female roles, and therefore that the performance of female characters involves the performance of femininity, facilitated by costumes (and complicated by cross-dressing roles); they may be less likely to consider that male actors performing male characters likewise involves the performance of masculinity. Likewise, students may be ready to discuss the performance of race in relation to Othello's or Aaron's blackness, but less familiar with discussing a character's whiteness. As Ambereen Dadabhoy observes, in Shakespeare studies 'the normative form of identity is white identity', and therefore 'part of the power of whiteness is that it's ever-present and also that it's invisible' (2021). Indeed, as Kim F. Hall argues in her seminal article 'Beauty and the Beast of Whiteness: Teaching Race and Gender', 'any discussion of race must deconstruct whiteness and not focus just on minoritized people' (1996, p. 461). Assisting students in 'seeing' whiteness and masculinity in relation to gender and race, rather than viewing male, white bodies as 'neutral' and 'invisible', can enable students to close read the gendered, racialised power structures in early modern texts.

Developing an understanding of racialised power structures can both inform students' historicised understanding of Shakespeare's plays, and be applied in contemporary social justice contexts. A fuller consideration of teaching Shakespeare and social justice (and teaching social justice through Shakespeare) is beyond the scope of this Element; important and necessary work on how to develop anti-racist pedagogy in the teaching of Shakespeare is available in recent books and online resources, and in the rich online discussions promoted under the #raceb4race and #Shakerace hashtags.[12] The focus of this Element is upon a historicised approach to Shakespeare, but of course teaching the past has contemporary political implications. While this Element does not explicitly focus upon these implications, this Element's embodied activities encourage students to reflect on the politics of embodiment in a way that can be applied both to early modern, and contemporary, power structures and ideologies. As the words of the student above suggest, reflecting on such politics offers a first step towards transforming them.

I end this introduction with the question with which I began: what are we teaching, when we teach Shakespeare?

This Element suggests that we are teaching plays that are shaped (and, indeed, co-authored) by the collaborative theatrical conditions in which they were first staged, and that situating these plays within their theatrical culture and alongside the works of other early modern dramatists can open up students' understandings of the plays themselves.

It suggests that we are teaching a form of professional entertainment which excludes the voices and performances (though not the presence or labours) of women; and that the voices and performances of women missing from the playhouse can be accessed through engagement with wider cultures of performance in early modern England.

It suggests that we are teaching plays that were shaped by, and themselves contributed to, the political ideologies of early modern England; and that by engaging with historical materials, not merely as contexts for the plays themselves, but as part of the wider cultural conversation, we can help make those ideologies visible to students, in all their contradictions and complexity.

It suggests that we are simultaneously teaching both literary texts and performance scripts, and that the method of embodied close reading proposed by this Element can enable students to close read Shakespeare's plays in relation to both literary analysis and performance: two interdependent

---

[12] See, for example, hooks, 1994; Hall, 1996; Brown, 2016; Thompson and Turchi, 2016, pp. 69–84; Blake, 2019; Eklund and Hyman, 2019; Arizona Center for Medieval and Renaissance Studies, 2021; Panjwani, 2022; and Dadabhoy and Mehdizadeh, 2023.

modes of analysis that can be accessed through the body, as my first section will show.

1 Teaching Shakespeare: Bodies and Spaces

When we teach a Shakespeare playtext, we teach a text designed for a particular spatial, multisensory, embodied performance context. As Farah Karim-Cooper and Tiffany Stern put it,

> Physical artefacts – the theatre and its props – together with the smell, sound and touch created by and for the environment, collectively made up the effects of performance ... [P]hysical and sensual theatre contributed to textual theatre. (2015, p. 1)

The sensual and embodied aspects of Shakespeare's plays have become central to Shakespeare criticism in recent years – from the smell of *Macbeth* (Gil Harris, 2007) to the tactility of *Antony and Cleopatra* (Edwards, 2020) – developing 'from a vibrant but somewhat marginal scholarly pursuit into a core area of inquiry' (Smith, 2020, p. 1). Yet despite the significance of these approaches to recent scholarship, Shakespeare's sensual theatre can be difficult to access in the classroom; as Alan C. Dessen writes, 'Shakespeare designed these playscripts for players, playgoers, and playhouses that no longer exist' (1999, p. 63). Attempts to draw student attention to the early modern theatrical experience are often, of necessity, textual: through the rich collection of eyewitness accounts of the playgoing experience in the appendices to Andrew Gurr's *Playgoing in Shakespeare's London* (2004), for example, or the full range of theatrical (and anti-theatrical) source materials in Tanya Pollard's *Shakespeare's Theater: A Sourcebook* (2004). The textual is sometimes supplemented by the material – visits to reconstructed theatres like Shakespeare's Globe, or to archaeological remains of early modern playhouses like the Rose Playhouse – or by the digital, such as the virtual reconstruction of the Rose,[13] or the Shakespeare's Globe 360 app, which

---

[13] See Ortelia Interactive Spaces, 2012; and Shakespearean London Theatres.

provides a virtual tour of the physical reconstructed playhouse.[14] 'Original practices' productions of early modern plays, whether experienced in person or via digital broadcasts or production recordings, can inform students' understanding of how specific early modern playing conditions interact with early modern playtexts (albeit in a very different cultural moment).[15]

This section suggests that an understanding of early modern theatre history is vital to understanding Shakespeare's plays. These plays were written for a particular performance context: from the soliloquies and asides that presuppose that an actor can see, in shared light, the audience they visibly address, to scenes requiring particular architectural features (from a visible stage door that exits to the tiring house to a balcony or a trapdoor), Shakespeare's plays are shaped by the performance conditions they assume. Furthermore, this section argues for an embodied, performance-based approach to teaching theatre history as a framework for Shakespeare's plays, not as an alternative to the resources described above, but as a complement to textual, material, and digital pedagogies. It offers three activities: the first enables an embodied approach to the past; the second, to theatre history; and the third builds on this theatre-historical approach to facilitate informed close readings of scenes from Shakespeare. In so doing, this section draws on recent pedagogical work on 'kinaesthetic', 'embodied', 'enactive', and 'open-space' learning.

The importance of incorporating movement into text-based learning activities to accommodate students with a kinaesthetic 'learning style' has long been acknowledged in pedagogical literature, though 'kinaesthetic' is often applied relatively broadly, as a 'perceptual preference related to the use of experience and practice (simulated or real)' (Fleming, 1992, p. 138). More recently, a wide range of disciplinary approaches have suggested the potential for a specifically embodied approach to teaching for all learners, regardless of learning

[14] Shakespeare's Globe. Thank you to Valerie Clayman Pie for sharing this app at Eleanor Rycroft's event on Early Modern Digital Practice, 16 December 2020.

[15] See Purcell, 2017.

style. 'Enactive' learning – learning by doing – has been explored as a means of enabling students to apply, and therefore grasp, abstract theoretical concepts (Gutierrez, 2019), while embodied learning has been shown to improve the long term-retention of new information (Wagner Cook, Mitchell, and Goldin-Meadow, 2008). Traci Lengel and Mike Kuczala suggest that incorporating movement into teaching activities allows 'the brain to process and consolidate new information' to 'improve retention', increases motivation, creates an 'exciting learning environment', and enables students 'to engage in a social environment' (2010, p. 10). The potential for kinaesthetic learning to enable consolidation of new information, and to create an exciting, social learning environment, is therefore particularly apt for teaching Shakespeare in relation to the playful, communal environment of the early modern playhouse.

The activities in this section offer a way to consolidate students' knowledge of theatre history through embodiment: they aim to make (what we know of) early modern England familiar to students, but also to enable students to grapple with the strangeness of Shakespearean playing conditions, and the ways in which they are alien to contemporary sensibilities more accustomed to proscenium arch or black box theatres. These activities demonstrate the potential for embodied, enactive, kinaesthetic learning in literary studies. In so doing, they suggest that the body is a particularly apt tool for thinking about texts themselves designed to be embodied, before an embodied audience, in the multisensory, social, playful early modern playhouse. In arguing this, I draw on the theory of 'open-space learning'.

'Open-space learning' (OSL) is an interdisciplinary pedagogical method chronicled by Monk et al. in 2011. The authors provide the case study of a third-year Shakespeare module, in which students are invited to choose a mode of study 'with chairs' (text-based), or 'without chairs' (practical); the latter enables 'the participant to become the producer and discoverer of knowledge' (p. 120). The students' 'real' physical engagement with the playtexts produces an embodied understanding of Shakespeare's plays – and their status as performance texts. The activities in this section borrow many elements of the OSL approach – the emphasis on a physical approach to the text; a sense of playfulness, experimentation, and risk; learning 'without chairs' – but they do so in a way that is designed to function in a traditional classroom or seminar context, and to be accessible to students who might not choose to take a module explicitly focused on a 'without chairs' approach, but who might nonetheless benefit from an embodied approach, when incorporated alongside more 'chair'-based textual analysis. OSL encourages a transformation of teaching space into 'theatrical space' in an explicit workshop context; in contrast, this section suggests the potential for any teaching space to become (or, indeed, to already function as) a theatrical space.

Ian Burrows writes of putting together a series of lectures concerning slapstick and tragedy which 'would require the students to think in detail about the demands made of the actor's body in various plays, as well as the audience's response to it':

> As I began to write these lectures it began to nag at me that – when I delivered them – I'd actually be presenting, in parallel, two transactions between performer and audience. While describing, say, a blind Gloucester falling down on stage in *King Lear*, I would be occupying a stage-space . . . in which I too was technically an actor and not simply an hour's worth of talk. (2020, p. 12)

Peter Brook famously describes the potential of any 'empty space' to become a 'bare stage': 'a man walks across this empty space whilst someone else is watching him, and this is all that is needed for an act of theatre to be engaged' (1968, p. 1). Burrows suggests that the modern lecture hall is itself already a theatrical space comprising an actor and an audience. The activities below draw on the potential of the classroom for a less explicitly hierarchical kind of performance, where, rather than becoming a passive audience to the active, authoritative lecturer, students can become actors *and* audience, taking ownership of teaching materials, and engaging as a group in collaborative theatre-making and close reading. I begin, crucially, with an activity where *all* the students are moving in the space simultaneously, but *not* as actors (in Brook's formulation, it is an empty space, but no-one is watching, because everyone is moving through it). This activity therefore allows students 'who may well be silent in lecture and seminar environments to have a voice' (Monk et al., 2011, p. 128). It also opens up possibilities for the democratisation of the teaching space, as students can literally take up space in a classroom that is not visually and spatially directed towards the teacher as the giver of knowledge, but rather, which enables the students to generate insights from their chosen space within the room.

I suggest that teachers seeking to use embodied learning in the classroom begin with Activity 1. This is a foundational activity which is designed to ground students in the concepts and approaches that underpin this Element. This activity asks students to imagine themselves as playgoers, and then to reflect on their own embodied identities. The follow-up activity suggests that students then move through space as a chosen Shakespeare character, in order to reflect on the ways in which the 'real' bodies of the early modern players would have interacted with the 'fictional' bodies of the characters. In moving between the 'real' and the 'imagined' – in the shift from the 'real' early modern playgoers to the fictional characters – students are experiencing, on a smaller scale, the central dynamic of this Element, which explores the relationship between the fictional worlds of Shakespeare's plays (and those of his sisters), and the embodied act of theatre-making. Each of the following activities asks students to engage with these shifts between the world of the play, the theatrical world of the playhouse, and the lived experiences of men and women in early modern England – and to consider the ways in which lived experiences inform theatrical performance, and themselves constitute a kind of performance. This activity therefore prepares students to undertake the activities that follow, in encouraging students to pay attention to the bodily, and to think about bodies performing on- and off-stage. In so doing, Activity 1 also prepares students to consider the significance of the all-white, all-male early modern playing companies, in relation to the range of bodies and identities these bodies performed onstage, and the ways in which this encouraged a sense of particular bodies as normative.

🎭 Activity 1: Playing with Bodies

Students are invited to imagine themselves as early modern playgoers. The classroom space should, insofar as is possible, be cleared of chairs and desks; alternatively, a corridor or outside space can be used. In preparation for this exercise, students should be made aware of the following:

(1) that Elizabethan sumptuary laws required clothing to reflect class distinctions.[16]

(2) that Elizabethan clothing shaped how men and women moved in the world: men, in form-fitting hose, could move more freely, while women, in large skirts, were more restricted, but could also take up more space.[17]

(3) that in early modern playhouses even productions set in another time or place would incorporate some elements of contemporary dress, which would shape movement.[18]

(4) that etiquette dictated that those of higher status could 'take the wall' (walk on the wall side of the road or pavement), while those of lower status must walk closer to the gutter.

Objectives

This activity will enable students to:

(1) understand how gender and status inform early modern clothing, and how this clothing shapes how bodies are interpreted

---

[16] Students can access these laws in The British Library, 'Elizabethan Dress Codes'.

[17] Students can view these distinctions by viewing portraits (see Bochicchio, 2020), and by watching a clip of Mark Rylance's Olivia in Shakespeare's Globe's *Twelfth Night*, 2013. Teachers can share anecdotes about women becoming stuck in doorways due to the size of their skirts (Bendall, 2019).

[18] See Henry Peacham's illustration of what appears to be a scene from William Shakespeare's *Titus Andronicus* (c. 1594–5), in which actors wear both Roman togas and doublet and hose, and the queen is dressed in what appears to be Elizabethan style.

(2) comprehend how clothing shaped how bodies moved in space, and how gender and status were performed through embodied motion

(3) experience gender and status, not as abstract concepts, but as the bedrock of social interactions

(4) apply an embodied understanding of these concepts to early modern playtexts and conditions of performance

Instructions

This activity invites students to imagine themselves as early modern playgoers. Students are asked to move through the space 'as men', and to think about the evidence from the portraits in considering how they do this (for example, in a world where shapely calves were prized, they might decide to display their legs in their walk). Students are then invited to move through the space 'as women', and to think about how the breadth of skirts might shape or constrain their movements. Then they are invited to choose which gender they would like to embody, and to choose their social status (monarch? nobleman or woman? gentleman or woman? clergyman? merchant? guild member? shopkeeper? servant? labourer? masterless man or woman?). Students are asked to move through space with their gender and status in mind, considering:

(a) How do they move through space? Where is their 'centre'? Which part of their body leads? How does clothing shape their movement? How might status?

(b) How do they interact with others? How do power and status operate as they move through the space?

Students for whom moving through the space is a barrier to participation can be, in pairs, invited to 'direct' other students in their movement; indeed, this can be used as an approach for the entire group, with half the students designated 'movers' and the other half 'directors'. All students are then invited to give feedback on their experience.

Then, students are invited to write, informally and reflectively, about their own intersecting identities (including gender, race, class, sexuality, disability, neurodiversity, etc.), and the ways these identities inform their own experiences of embodiment. Students should then reflect on their experience of moving in space as early modern men and women, and how this was informed by their own identities. This writing is private, and does not feed into any formal form of assessment; its role is to prepare students to take an embodied, historicised approach to early modern texts by encouraging self-conscious reflection on the significance of embodiment in relation to performed identity. Students can be invited (but should not be required) to share reflections with the wider group.

Follow-Up Activity: Playing Shakespeare's Characters

Students are invited to move through space as actors onstage, choosing their own roles either in a particular Shakespeare play being studied by the group, or in any Shakespeare play. For the purposes of this exercise, several students can, if they wish, choose the same 'role', and they do not need to reveal their role to each other. Again, students are invited to consider how they move through the space, which parts of their bodies might lead, how power and status operate in the ways in which they make space for others (whose identity they may or may not guess through their movement). Students then share their chosen character, and how they experienced this exercise, in a group discussion. They are invited to reflect on the ways in which the 'real' bodies of the (all-white, all-male) early modern players would have interacted with the 'fictional' bodies of the characters.

As Nedda Mehdizadeh puts it, interrogating early modern power structures can offer an opportunity to think *with* our students about 'the power structures [that] guide our everyday lives' and 'what role we play in those power structures (whether we're aware of it or not)' – and how these power structures interact with our bodies (Arizona Center for Medieval and Renaissance

Studies, 2021). In Activity 1, by moving their body in space while performing an identity that is not their own, students can gain an embodied understanding of these intersecting identities that they can then bring to bear on early modern texts, in which particular identities – male, white, able-bodied identities – can become normative and therefore invisible.[19] This activity equips students to interrogate the historicised power structures embedded in Shakespeare's plays, as well as to apply this understanding of power structures to their own embodied experiences. Beginning with this activity enables students to situate their understanding of Shakespeare's plays, in the context of early modern culture, in relation to their own, embodied experience of a world that is still shaped by early modern ideologies. It also makes visible what is at stake when teaching Shakespeare, if teachers unthinkingly replicate the power structures that shape the society to which his plays are responding.

The following activity shifts from the interactions between broader societal contexts and playhouse contexts to focus more specifically on how theatrical contexts shape Shakespeare's playtexts. This activity offers students the opportunity to experience the spatial dynamics of an early modern playhouse from the perspective of a performer, making the class-room, as Ralph Cohen puts it, into a 'rough miniature of an Elizabethan theatre' (1999, p. 81). In so doing, it offers a framework for close reading Shakespeare's plays, particularly in relation to direct address to the audience: this activity is designed to enable students to understand the distinction between (in Robert Weimann's model) the '*locus*' and the '*platea*' – the imagined world of the play, and the world of the playhouse where characters can speak to the audience – or, as Weimann puts it:

> [the] distinction between the *locus* as a fairly specific imaginary locale or self-contained space in the world of the play and the *platea* as an opening in mise-en-scène through which the place and time of the stage-as-stage and the cultural occasion itself are made either to assist or resist the socially and verbally elevated, spatially and temporally remote representation. (2000, p. 181)

---

[19] On Shakespeare and bodily norms, see Iyengar, 2014; and Loftis, 2021.

This quotation can be difficult for students to grasp on first reading; an embodied demonstration of 'socially and verbally elevated, spatially and temporally remote representation' (an elite character, such as Hamlet, addressing another character in the fictional time and place of the play) versus 'the place and time of the stage-as-stage' (the playhouse in which Hamlet can directly address the audience) can help students to comprehend how direct address in asides and soliloquies creates a bridge between the remote world of the play and the here-and-now of the audience. Such direct address may 'assist' us in believing in the world of the play (by bringing us in), or it may 'resist' the illusion by reminding us that we live in another time and place altogether. These concepts can be introduced to the students either in advance of participating in the activity, or in a period of reflective discussion following the activity; the activity itself is designed to enable students to experience these concepts in practice.

☺ Activity 2: Playing the Player

The key preparatory information for students is as follows:[20]

(1) the layout of the stage (the stage doors, upper stage, and shape of the stage; the trapdoors above and below; the associations of the canopy over the stage with 'the heavens', and of the area beneath the stage with 'hell')
(2) the layout of the playhouse audience (the yard, the galleries, etc.), and the cost, advantages, and pitfalls of the various audience positions
(3) the fact of 'shared light': the actors and audience can see one another, illuminated by daylight (in an outdoor playhouse) or candlelight (in an indoor playhouse)

---

[20] This information can be found in Stern, 2004, ch. 2. For a brief open-access summary, see Zafar-Arif, 2016; and Shakespeare Birthplace Trust. See also Shakespeare's Globe 360 app.

Students may also find it helpful to gain physical or digital experience of the architecture of early modern playhouses in advance of participating in this activity, by using the digital aids suggested above, or viewing a toy 'pop-up' theatre (e.g. Forward, 2005). This activity can take place in a classroom; it simply requires an 'empty space' which is large enough to become a stage space for at least half of the cohort, a further empty space that can represent the yard (but where it may make sense for 'groundlings' to be seated, rather than standing, to enable sightlines for all), and chairs arranged in an informal semi-circle that roughly maps onto the 'gallery' space behind. If there is space, all participants can be invited to be 'players' simultaneously (with an imagined audience); if not, one half of the cohort can function as players and the other half as audience, and then the two positions can be reversed.

Objectives

This activity will enable students to:

(1) understand how direct address to the audience operates in the shared light conditions of an early modern playhouse
(2) comprehend the distinction between direct address to the audience (in asides or soliloquies) and dialogue, oration, and asides between characters
(3) apply the concepts of *locus* and *platea* in an early modern playhouse context
(4) analyse textual examples in relation to these concepts

Instructions

This is an activity of two halves – first, the 'actors' walk around the stage space, speaking to each other. Whenever they encounter another actor, one says, 'To be or not to be?', and the other responds, 'That is the question'. If a student is unable to move through the playing space, they can participate from a chosen place in the playing space by addressing other students as they pass.

Then, the actors speak the same line in its entirety – 'To be or not to be, that is the question' – to the imagined audience in an early modern playhouse space. They should then point at the section of the audience to which they chose to address their line, and be invited comment on their choice: Did they speak to a particular (imagined or real) audience member, and if so, was it a groundling, someone in a lord's box, or someone in the gallery? Or did they address their line to a larger section of the audience? Were they looking up (towards the heavens, and the canopy above) or down (towards hell, and to the trapdoor below)? Did they gesture? Ask them to recite the line again, and to make a different choice. How might this change their delivery, and their engagement with the audience?

Follow-Up Activity: *Locus* and *Platea* in *Romeo and Juliet*

Detailed attention to a fuller textual example can help to further develop students' understandings of the relationship between *locus* and *platea*. For example, the balcony scene in *Romeo and Juliet* (II. ii) features a character talking aloud to an imagined person (Juliet to Romeo); a character talking to the audience (Romeo in his asides); two characters talking to each other onstage (Romeo and Juliet); and one onstage character talking to an offstage character, whose voice breaks the boundary between the onstage and offstage worlds (Juliet and the Nurse). Asking students to identify who each character is addressing, and how this affects the relationship between the imagined world of the play and the 'real' world of the playhouse, can open up the relationship between the *locus* and the *platea* in concrete terms. This task, at its most basic, enables students to differentiate between the fact that Juliet is addressing an imagined Romeo (not Romeo himself), while Romeo addresses first the audience, and then Juliet directly. A more complex discussion can take account of gender roles in relation to Juliet's liminal position at the boundaries of her home, and Romeo's ability to move freely, to trespass in the garden of an enemy, and to speak to the audience directly.[21]

This brief activity gives students the opportunity to do several things: to reflect on the distinction between dialogue (as addressing, and listening to, other characters) and asides and soliloquies (in which characters might talk to themselves, or directly address the audience);[22] to explore how a line might change when embodied spatially in different ways; and to consider the multiplicity of the early modern audience and how spatial arrangements might shape audience engagement – does a groundling, in close proximity to the stage, engage with an actor differently from someone viewing the stage from their seat in the upper gallery? The follow-up activity enables students to apply their embodied understanding of asides and soliloquies, and of the distinction between *locus* and *platea*, to particular textual examples.

Activities 1 and 2 are extra-textual; they invite students to explore the lived realities and theatrical conditions that informed Shakespeare's play-texts, and then offer ways of applying these realities and conditions to Shakespeare's playtexts, enabling a theatrically informed mode of reading. We turn now to ways of bringing embodiment directly to Shakespeare's plays, by exploring the playtext in performance.

🎭 Activity 3: Staging the Scene

This activity can be applied to a short extract from any Shakespeare play. The example extract I give here is the opening few lines of *Hamlet*: from Bernardo's 'Who's there?' to Francisco's repetition of the same

---

[21] This activity was inspired by conversations with Philip Bird. On gender and space in this scene, see Whipday, 2019a, pp. 120–1; and A Bit Lit, 2020b (an open-access video).

[22] On the 'inherent tension in a soliloquy as to who exactly is being addressed', see Palfrey, 2011, pp. 270–2.

phrase (I.i.1–14).[23] This opening offers a masterclass in playwriting: Shakespeare briefly and concisely establishes the place, time, and atmosphere of his play-world, creating the midnight world of the castle where the king's soldiers are cold, 'sick at heart', and afraid. We see how the same phrase can be differently weighted by audience expectation by the second time it is uttered; after hearing the first few lines we, like Bernardo and Francisco, know that it is midnight, cold, and silent, and we wait, with the soldiers, for the newcomers to speak and reveal their identity.

These lines also offer a concise but rich example of how Shakespeare's text interacts with playhouse conditions.[24] As for the previous activity, students need to be aware of playhouse architecture and the significance of 'shared light'. It is also necessary for students to be made aware of the following:

(1) the 'bare' stage: the lack of set, and the consequent significance of costumes and (occasionally) props
(2) the lack of amplified sound or underscoring music; the use of offstage musicians only in act breaks or when called for by the text
(3) the fact that plays were designed for particular performance conditions, but they were also designed to be flexible in terms of performance spaces, travelling between outdoor playhouses, court, touring spaces (in inns and town halls), and, sometimes, indoor playhouses and/or country houses

Students do not need to be familiar with *Hamlet*, but they should be informed that it was written for an open-air playhouse (the Globe), and that it was also flexible enough to be performed inside at court (and, eventually, at Blackfriars) and both outside and inside on tour (at inns and town halls). It is therefore a play that opens in darkness, designed for performance conditions where the stage is lit (whether by daylight or by candlelight). The darkness, then, like the fear and (perhaps) the cold, is imaginary, created in the interplay between the words of the

---

[23] All references to Shakespeare's plays are to the New Cambridge editions.

[24] For resources on these playing conditions, see footnote 9.

playwright, the performances (and costumes/props) of the actors, and the imaginations of the audience. Staging this scene can help students to think about the possible cues for performance encoded in an early modern playtext, how these can be unlocked in relation to a specific performance context, and how these might inform a 'literary' reading of a scene.

Objectives

This activity will enable students to:

(1) identify moments in the text that provide instructions to actors and 'cue' performance choices
(2) apply relevant concepts from theatre history (e.g. costume; theatrical architecture; shared light)
(3) make informed choices about how to perform the scene
(4) analyse the text in relation to these performance possibilities

Instructions

Divide students into pairs, and give each pair the first fourteen lines of *Hamlet*. Each pair of students must find a different section of the classroom in which to 'rehearse'; chairs and desks can be moved to one side, or students can rehearse in the aisles if need be. Each pair of students must assign the two roles, and read these lines aloud. You can ask them, when doing so, to be alert to any cues for performance – students can think of these as clues as to how the original actors may have performed these parts. Students can be encouraged to pay attention to the creation of place, time, mood, and character, and also to any references to props, costumes, or gestures. They may also find it useful to think about the sensory experiences of the characters – what do the characters see and hear (and feel)? How does this map on, or not map on, to what an audience can see or hear in a 'shared light' playhouse? It is helpful if the students can refer to scholarly notes for the extract, to help them gloss phrases like 'unfold yourself'.

Next students put the scene 'on its feet', acting it out as a pair (all students should do this simultaneously, so that none feel 'on show'). They are encouraged to think about what choices they have to make – where does the scene provide instructions for movement, physicality, emotions? When are props or costume required? What are the dynamics between the characters? What information do they need to convey to the audience? Any students uncomfortable doing this, or unable to do this, can read the scene aloud and make these decisions without putting them into practice.

Volunteers can then be invited to perform for the group. As the extract is very brief, two or three performances can be productive, to enable students to see how, with the same cues, choices or interpretations might differ; this can provide both insights and challenges for the theatre historian, while opening up potential readings for the literary scholar. Students should talk through the logic of these choices, with other students invited to share their own choices, enabling a collaborative group reading of some of the performance features of the text.

There are a few cues (or clues) that students might notice:

- Bernardo's initial question, 'Who's there?' This could suggest that he sees someone, but he cannot tell that this someone is Francisco. Or it could suggest that he <u>hears</u> someone, but it is too dark to see him (at least at a distance). It therefore tells an audience at a daylit performance that the scene they are watching is in the dark.
- The first half of Francisco's line – 'Nay, answer me!' – offers a momentary power struggle between the characters, concerning who has the right to demand information of the other. The mystery implied by the initial unanswered question may be identified in the creation of a tense atmosphere (Frank, 2019).
- Students editions are likely to explain that Francisco's line, 'Stand and unfold yourself' refers to Francisco's cloak. This line, then, is

a performance cue, asking Francisco to reveal his uniform beneath the cloak, or to drop his hood to make his face visible, or both.

- ''Tis now struck twelve' tells us the time, and confirms that the scene takes place in darkness. Students might think of the associations of midnight, in relation to ghost stories or the 'witching time of night' (III. ii.359).
- Bernardo's 'get thee to bed, Francisco' is another instruction (more colloquial and intimate than 'Stand and unfold yourself'), and is not immediately obeyed. Students may discuss whether to begin to exit 'to bed' and then turn back for their next line, or to ignore the instruction.
- ''Tis bitter cold' gives us information that may inform the actors' physicality – do the students shiver, or clutch cloaks around them? 'I am sick at heart' is another clue as to the atmosphere of the scene.
- Students may remark that Bernardo's 'Bid them make haste' suggests that, despite his dismissal of Francisco, he doesn't wish to be left alone – a clue to the fact that he seems to be afraid, which can be shown physically.
- Francisco's 'I think I hear them' reminds us again of the senses, and the fact that the newcomers can be heard but not seen. Coupled with the fact that there is 'not a mouse stirring', students might note that Francisco is straining to hear unexpected noises in the silence.
- The repeated 'Who's there?' reminds us of the darkness and Francisco's fear, cranking up the tension. Students might remark that as readers, we know the identities of these new characters from the stage directions, but the characters do not – and nor does the audience (especially if these characters are cloaked, though Marcellus' clothing may mark him out as a sentinel).

Of course, not all students will arrive at all of these insights and possibilities – each student group might come up with one or two, enough to open up a productive discussion about, for example, staging, darkness, the senses, atmosphere, or power dynamics in this scene – or to prepare students for a fuller exploration of the Ghost in *Hamlet* in relation to the remainder of the scene. This activity should enable students to think about how theatre history might inform a close reading of a playtext.

Follow-Up Activity: Knocking at the Gates in *Macbeth*

Once students have gained confidence in close reading a brief extract through performance, this activity can be applied to any scene from a Shakespeare play. II.ii in *Macbeth* offers particularly rich material for this approach. Students can be asked to perform the scene, as Lady Macbeth and Macbeth, in pairs, or two student volunteers can perform this before the entire class, with the rest of the group pausing the scene whenever a performance cue is identified, or a decision is required. Students can be encouraged to build on the previous activities to look out for particular performative and sensory features: for example, Macbeth and Lady Macbeth's direct address to the audience in the scene; entrances and exits; the bloody daggers (and the point at which they become visible); the imagined darkness in this night-time scene; the sudden sounds that break the night's silence (the shriek of the owl, the knocking). Students should then be invited to reflect on the effect of this in creating the tension of the scene and the audience's complicity with the Macbeths in the immediate aftermath of the murder.[25]

The aforementioned activities are enactive: they require students to act, to make choices in relation to particular textual features. They are embodied: they require students to respond to the text, and to each other, with their bodies in space. They draw on, and consolidate, an understanding of theatre history. They are social, requiring students to interact with one another; playful, in enabling students to interact with the playtext in unexpected, physical ways; and non-hierarchical, offering students the opportunity to gain authority and generate knowledge about the playtext through making embodied choices.

[25] See Lewis and Whipday, 2019; some of these ideas are discussed in A Bit Lit, 2020a (an open-access video).

These embodied, enactive, performance-based activities are specifically designed for a literature classroom. While these activities can offer a range of pedagogical benefits – an understanding of theatre history, of the daily performance of gender and status in early modern England, and of how Shakespeare's playtexts function in performance – their primary aim is to enable students to apply Shakespeare's performance contexts to Shakespeare's playtexts, and to close read Shakespeare's plays. They are designed to encourage students to apply theatre-historical and societal concepts; to identify textual features; and to analyse these features, analysis which can be developed in relation to the play as a whole. In short, they assist students in developing the skills and close textual engagement required in literary study. In so doing, they create a social, exciting, playful, embodied learning environment that encourages students to reflect on the rich and multi-sensory world of early modern playhouses that shaped the plays they study.

This section has explored how reading Shakespeare's plays as theatre might be taught through an embodied approach to playhouse history; but an embodied approach to teaching Shakespeare need not be restricted to professional playhouse contexts. How might further social, political, and cultural histories – of gender, of power, of performance – that intersect with the plays of Shakespeare be taught through embodiment? The next section offers one possible answer to this question: through teaching the lost or neglected performances, storytelling, and writing of Shakespeare's sisters.

2 Teaching Shakespeare's Sisters

How do we teach Shakespeare's sisters, the women who created theatre in early modern England? In 2007, Karen Raber writes of Woolf's 'Judith Shakespeare':

> Woolf's character, originally intended to draw attention to the absence of women from the canon . . . has unfortunately gone a long way towards convincing a couple of generations of undergraduates that there simply weren't *any* women poets or dramatists in Shakespeare's day. (2007, p. 21)

Today's undergraduates should face no such fate. Decades of feminist scholarship have uncovered a wealth of female authors who can be taught alongside the male early modern canon, and are rapidly coming to constitute a canon of their own (May, 2021). Women writers and translators of prose and poetry abound: Anne Bradstreet, Margaret Cavendish, Aemilia Lanyer, Anne Locke, Katherine Philips, Hester Pulter, Mary Sidney, Rachel Speght, Elizabeth Tudor, Isabella Whitney, and Mary Wroth, among others. There is also a rich range of female dramatists (a list in which Sidney and Wroth again feature): Elizabeth Cary (as the earliest female writer of an original, printed play in English); Jane Lumley and Mary Sidney (as translators of male-authored plays); the prolific Margaret Cavendish; Mary Wroth (whose play *Love's Victory* survives in manuscript), and, of course, Aphra Behn, the first female professional playwright in English.

For those teaching Shakespeare and his contemporaries, and therefore focused on writers of drama within the Elizabethan and Jacobean periods, the opportunity for including the works of women writers is far more limited – incorporating Cary's *The Tragedy of Mariam*, Sidney's translation of *The Tragedie of Antonie*, and Wroth's *Love's Victory*. Each of these plays is a 'closet drama': unlike the plays written for the professional playhouses in the previous section, these were plays written to be read, or perhaps privately performed. The female playwrights listed here are noblewomen, reflective of the limited opportunities for literacy (and the yet more limited opportunities for classical education) for all but the few elite women for whom an unnecessary, expensive education was a form of conspicuous consumption by their male relatives (Purkiss, 1998, p. xv). The teaching of these authors alongside Shakespeare has the advantage of putting female voices in con-versation with a canonical male voice, but it has the disadvantage of offering only the voices of those from a very particular class. Furthermore, closet dramas can look unfamiliar to readers used to the conventions of commercial drama; they privilege rhetorically complex speech over dramatic action. Teaching closet dramas alongside plays for the professional stage can involve positioning male creativity as popular, professional, and presented in a dramatic form recognisable to us today, while (potentially) implying that female creativity was elite, exclusive, marginal, and presented in a form that students may find alienating. Such a strategy, then, is positive in providing students with a more 'inclusive' cultural history – as Susanne Woods and Margaret Hannay put it, 'any account of the tradition of writers in English must speak of all writers, not just male writers' (2000, p. 3) – but risks reinscribing the assumptions that led Woolf to invent 'Shakespeare's sister' who died and left no writing behind her.

This section offers a broader approach to exploring the voices and creativity of both elite and non-elite women in Shakespeare's time. Wendy Wall suggests that 'we are only beginning to appreciate the ideologically capacious spectrum of literacies and writings in which female subjects participated' (2016, p. 22). Peter Davidson and Jane Stevenson offer the term 'devisership' to enable us to expand 'what constitutes a cultural intervention to consider works that communicate a woman's intentions without necessarily being created by her own hand' (2007, pp. - 223–4). I argue that this concept of 'devisership' can enable us to apply Wall's 'capacious' approach to early modern theatre-making, which explores female playwrights alongside female performers, female patrons, and traces of lost female voices in other kinds of texts, enabling us to recover a range of women's cultural interventions beyond those of the elite and educated.

This section, then, offers a way teaching a wider range of female voices alongside Shakespeare, through a more capacious understanding of how an early modern English 'performance text' might be defined. An early modern play, written for the professional stage, is potentially both a prompt for, and a record of, a performance; the provenances of surviving printed playtexts range from authorial manuscripts that are designed to be realised in performance; playhouse manuscripts, which offer a text for future performances as well a potential culminative record of past performances; and memorial texts reconstructed from the memories or parts of actors, or the note-taking of audience members, which offer a record of a particular performance – or some combination of the above.[26] I suggest that female performance in masques, closet dramas, and household entertainments can be taught

---

[26] See for example Jowett, 2007, pp. 99–120. Scholarly debates around these issues are ongoing, and textual provenance is usually a matter of scholarly interpretation.

alongside the 'all male stage'; records of these performances, as accessed through surviving performance texts and other kinds of archival evidence, allow students to engage with a wider range of female theatricality activity.

Furthermore, the cultural activities of elite women can be taught alongside performance texts that offer records of the voices of non-elite women. Printed witch trial accounts, along with other kinds of court records, offer direct access to transcriptions of oral storytelling by non-elite early modern women. Although these records are of course shaped by the questions asked, and mediated by the scribe recording the words of the speaker, they nonetheless provide a record of a spoken performance before an audience – which might be composed of only the interrogator and the scribe, or of a wider public. Such documents therefore meet the above definition of a 'performance text'.[27] As Laura Gowing has observed:

> Contemporary culture held a stock of stories in both oral and printed form whose contexts, events, and results could be rifled for the tales told in everyday life, in the moments of dispute, and at court. The depositions that survive in the church court records ... are both individual and typical, innovative and repetitive. (1996, p. 58)

Depositions at court, then, are non-literary, yet they are, like any literary text, at once derivative and original, generic and creative. Furthermore, as Diane Purkiss argues (1996), witch trials enabled the female accused to create narratives, 'shaping their own stories' (p. 145) in 'an occasion for female self-fashioning' (p. 162). These printed trial accounts, like Gowing's 'stock of stories', both built on, and contributed to, the wider cultural conversation, enabling a literature of the illiterate, wherein women accused of witchcraft (and their 'witnesses' and 'victims') drew on generic tropes to construct original narratives.[28]

---

[27] See also Brannen, 2006; Brannen notes that teaching church court records in drama classes can 'illustrate for my students how difficult it is to define "drama"' (p. 87).

[28] I am grateful to Ruth Connolly for the phrase 'literature of the illiterate'.

Teaching a wider range of performance texts also offers students a richer understanding of early modern theatre history. The version of theatre history that focuses on plays written for the professional stage is, of necessity, a version of theatre history that privileges male authorship, male performance, male creativity. It also tends to focus on the performance contexts of purpose-build playhouses, which presuppose a London audience. Engaging with a wider range of performance contexts offers students a feminist form of historical recovery, as well as a much fuller picture of how men and women in early modern England engaged with performance beyond the capital – a participatory model in which theatre-making was not limited to a professional few.

There are further pedagogical benefits to teaching women's writing, and the broader history of women's creativity, through performance. As the Introduction suggested, the significance of performance as a mode for teaching Shakespeare has long been recognised in school classrooms, while any school or university student approaching a well-known Shakespearean play will have access to a considerable performance tradition, incorporating local professional and amateur performances, recorded productions, live streamings, reviews, photographs, film and television adaptations, and pop cultural appropriations. Shakespeare is conceived of as performed and performable; as simultaneously a revered 'dead' playwright (carrying the weight of canonicity and literary authority), and a 'live' one, continually re-staged and re-imagined. In contrast, the women whose creativity is explored in this section are often taught – if they are taught at all – in relation to literary recovery, as at once dead and all-but-forgotten. Teaching early modern women writers and performers in an embodied way offers students an opportunity to engage with these women as 'live'. Affording female theatre-makers this kind of attention, with our voices and our bodies, breaks – or perhaps, remakes – canonical boundaries, enabling early modern female creativity to take up space in the classroom as well as on the bookshelf.

Situating female voices and performances alongside the plays of Shakespeare also benefits students' ability to analyse female (and indeed, male) characters in Shakespeare, by complicating their understanding of early modern gender roles. It can be tempting for students to read gender politics of both Shakespeare's plays and the early modern past in relation to a straightforward model of female oppression (focusing on examples of shamed, silenced, and murdered women, from Hero to Desdemona), or alternatively, in relation to a proto-feminist model of 'empowerment' (focusing on 'strong' women, such as Lady Macbeth or Volumnia).[29] Exploring female-authored texts – and recreating female performances – enables students to speak back to the male-authored female characters that so often dominate discussions of early modern femininity, and offers a more nuanced picture of how men and women in early modern England experienced gender and power, both socio-politically and in performance.

The activities below, perhaps surprisingly for a section on 'Shakespeare's Sisters', all focus on male-authored texts – these are texts that were performed by women, that were commissioned by women, that recorded female voices, but they were not written by women. The reasons for this decision are two-fold. The first is that, as I have outlined above, this section seeks to expand the range of texts that can be studied in relation to women as theatre-makers, and therefore focuses on examples that, I argue, recover female creativity in unexpected places. The second reason is more dispiriting; I have tried, throughout this volume, to focus on plays that are available online, in open-access editions, or are available in affordable paperback editions (or in many cases, both). Finding such editions of plays authored by women is a challenge, since they are currently either prohibitively expensive (Lady Mary Wroth's *Love's Victory*) or out of print (Lady Jane Lumley's *Iphigenia*); one exception is Elizabeth Cary's *The Tragedy of Mariam* (and performance-based activities involving this play are discussed at length in Maguire, 2002).[30] I have therefore focused the activities in this section on texts that both expand the range of materials students can study in relation to female theatre-making, and are easily

---

[29] These challenges were discussed by school teachers and academics at the RSA 'Innovative High School Teaching of Renaissance Studies' Webinar, 4 June 2021.

[30] At the time of this book's going to press, a more affordable paperback edition of *Love's Victory* has become available in autumn 2022 (Findlay ed.).

accessible online, while including some follow-up activities that can be applied to female-authored plays.

These activities, like those in the previous section, are embodied, and draw on kinaesthetic, enactive, and OSL pedagogies. They also offer an additional approach: the recovery of female voices, and the recreation and reimagining of their performances, involves not just embodiment, but also creativity. Students are asked to engage with these texts as theatre-makers themselves, making creative choices about re-performing and re-imagining these texts. While such creativity in the classroom has value in and of itself (Jackson et al., 2006), I suggest that this creativity has particular value as a tool for literary analysis. Creative activities have long been used in Shakespeare classrooms, though the shift to recognising creative literary criticism has been more recent; in 2019, Rob Conkie and Scott Maisano both noted and promoted the increasing recognition of 'creative criticism', or '*literary creaticism*' (2019, p. 3).[31] I argue that, just as making directorial and actorly choices forces students to read closely in order to find the moments in the text that signal or suggest such a choice, and to interpret these textual details (of which more in Activity 5), so engaging creatively with the text requires attentiveness to language and imagery (as I show in Activity 4), and to questions of voice and narrative structure (as I demonstrate in Activity 6). This section, then, proposes both a mode of historically-informed imaginative recovery, through which students engage with the performances and voices of early modern women, and a method of creative, embodied close reading that opens up literary analysis of the texts in question.

Masques

📖 What Is a Masque?

A masque was a multimedia performance that incorporated music, spectacle (often involving elaborate set design, costumes, and stage effects), dancing, singing, and a performed text. Masques were elite,

---

[31] See also Corbett, Kisby Compton, and Pooley, 2022; and Bertolet and Levin, 2018.

exclusive, private performances, usually at court; they featured professional (all-male) actors in spoken and sung parts, and members of the
court (both men and women) in roles involving spectacle and dance.
Masques ended in a dance performed by the entire court, in what we
might now think of as immersive theatre, as the audience joined the
masquers in dancing. The masque was often preceded by an anti-
masque performed by the professional actors, in which forces of dis-
order and disruption were invoked, only to be banished by the forces of
good in the masque itself.

Court masques were an opportunity for an extremely select number of elite
women to perform in public (albeit an exclusive public), and could also be
an opportunity for female devisership; at the Jacobean court, Queen Anne
commissioned a number of masques from writers like Samuel Daniel and
Ben Jonson, in which she and her ladies performed. The activity below uses
Jonson's *Masque of Queens*, commissioned by Anne and performed by Anne
and her ladies before her husband King James, as a way for students to
engage with female performance in masque culture. This activity is developed from my experience of directing *Masque of Queens* (produced by
Daniel Starza Smith and Nadine Akkerman) at New College Chapel,
Oxford, as part of a conference on Lucy Harington Russell, Countess of
Bedford, who danced in the masque's first performance in 1609. The
production recording is freely available online (Appendix 4: Jonson).

🎭 Activity 4: Tableaux: Witches and Queens

Ben Jonson's *Masque of Queens* offers two modes of performed femininity:
transgressive, disruptive, dangerous witches in the anti-masque (performed – and voiced – by male actors); and heroic, idealised, regal queens
in the masque (performed – in silence – by female noblewomen). Inviting
students to stage these two versions of femininity can enable them to
explore the significance of female performance in the masque, and how
this contrasts with the way the male actors perform dangerous femininity
as the witches – the tensions between, as Clare McManus puts it, 'the

bodies of the courtly women and the professional male player' performing 'alternating versions of femininity' (2008, p. 455). Students should be shown images of Inigo Jones' costumes and set design in advance, to give them a sense of the expensive, multi-sensory entertainment afforded by the masque, and how the text and visual effects interacted in the creation of the performance.[32] An open-access, original spelling edition of the manuscript of *Masque of Queens* is available online (Jonson, 1692).

Objectives

This activity will enable students to:

(1) understand how early modern masques functioned, and the relationship between the masque and the antimasque
(2) identify the language and imagery used to describe female characters in *Masque of Queens*
(3) analyse how this imagery functions in the fictional world of the masque
(4) explore how this imagery can be embodied by performers
(5) comprehend how the gender of the early modern performers shaped the power dynamics of the masque in performance

Instructions

This activity invites students to create two tableaux (still, unmoving images) with their bodies: one in which they perform the eleven witches (ruled over by a 'Dame'), and the other in which they perform the eleven queens (ruled over by Queen Anne). When the Dame greets the eleven witches she rules, she names and describes each one as the personification of a particular vice (see Appendix 1 Extract 1):

> First, then, advance

[32] See for example The British Library, 1609; and Jones, 1609a, 1609b.

> My drowsy servant, stupid Ignorance,
> Known by thy scaly vesture; and bring on
> Thy fearful Sister, wild Suspicion,
> Whose eyes do never sleep; Let her knit hands
> With quick Credulity, that next her stands,
> Who hath but one ear, and that always ope[n]. . .

How can the open ear of Credulity, the unsleeping eyes of Suspicion, or the scaly vesture and drowsiness of Ignorance, be embodied? Students are placed in pairs, and each pair is assigned a personification, which they will embody, either in a two-person tableaux, or, if need be, a one-person tableaux (with one student acting, the other directing). Each pair can then demonstrate their tableau to the group as a whole, while the teacher reads the passage aloud, indicating the relevant tableau. This can open up a discussion about how Jonson describes each personification (often in relation to a single body part, many of these associated with a particular sense), and can help to remind students, when reading the masque, that each element is designed to be both voiced and embodied, as a visual and aural spectacle.

Next, students are given the eleven queens to embody (in the same pairs), according to Jonson's descriptions. Students will often have only a single adjective to respond to, such as 'swift-foot Camilla', or 'victorious Thomyris' (see Appendix 2 Extract 2). Students are invited to compare the experience of embodying these descriptions to embodying the witches. Then, students can be invited to watch the production of *Masque of Queens*, and discuss the characterisation of the twelve witches (Figure 1) and twelve queens in relation to the wider plot, in which the witches attempt to destroy the 'soft peace' of the court, but are banished by the very sound of the queens' 'fame'. This can open up a discussion about the complexities of Jonson's portrayal of 'virtuous' and 'dangerous' womanhood: the queens are silenced and yet they are also authoritative, powerful, and, in some cases, military; while the witches are disruptive, offering a topsy-turvy version of femininity and threatening the safety of James's court, yet they are failures, struggling to call up their Dame

Figure 1 Charlotte Fletcher, Melanie Rio, Shana Krisiloff, Emory Noakes, Emma Harris, and Elspeth North as the witches in *Masque of Queens*, directed by Emma Whipday, produced by Nadine Akkerman and Daniel Starza Smith (2016), New College Chapel: still from performance recording © King's College London

and never succeeding in their spell to produce a fire-breathing drakes. Students can then discuss the significance of female noblewomen silently performing the roles of these queens, following the disruptive, vocal, theatrical performances of femininity in the antimasque.

Follow-Up Activity: Lady Rachel Fane's May Masque

Court masques offer an opportunity to explore female performance and devisership, but not female authorship. Masques written by women do survive, but these are explicitly produced in the context of household performance; for example, Lady Rachel Fane's *May Masque* (1627; written when Fane was just fourteen) offers a short, site-specific performance that features direct address to family members who were within the original audience (spoken by the male characters that people Fane's masque). Staging Fane's *May Masque* can offer students the opportunity to explore an example of a teenage girl's creativity and authorial agency, and to discuss how familial relationships could be negotiated through performance.[33]

Closet Drama

📖 What Is Closet Drama?

'Closet drama' is a term used to describe plays that were not designed to be performed in a professional context (Straznicky, 2004, p. 1). Closet dramas usually follow the neoclassical conventions of unity of place and time (with plays set in a single location, over a single day). They often feature lengthy and rhetorically complex speeches, with limited action onstage, and descriptions of action that occurs off-stage, as well as a Chorus, who comments directly on characters' choices. Recent scholarship has argued for the performability of closet drama, overturning assumptions that closet drama was a genre written to be read rather than staged; surviving evidence suggests these plays may have been performed in private, household productions.[34]

Closet drama offers the opportunity to explore the theatrical agency of elite women, through authorship, deviership, and female performance. The activity involves staging a scene from a closet drama: the premise of this activity is that closet drama is stageable, but it does not require the assumption that closet drama *was staged*; rather, it explores the *potential* staging implicit in the text itself. The example given here is Samuel Daniel's

---

[33] Staging Fane's *Masque* in a teaching context was modelled by Ariane Balizet at my workshop on 'Resurrecting Shakespeare (and His Sisters)' at the SAA Annual Meeting, 2014.

[34] See for example Findlay, 2006.

The Tragedie of Cleopatra, which gives students the opportunity to explore female performance. My colleague Yasmin Arshad discovered a link between a lost portrait of a Jacobean noblewoman dressed as Cleopatra, and Daniel's play: a surviving photograph from a 1948 Christie's catalogue shows that the portrait displays one of Cleopatra's speeches from the 1607 edition of the play, on what seems to be an actors' 'part'. Arshad has plausibly identified the woman in this (now lost) portrait as Lady Anne Clifford, who performed as the Egyptian queen Berenice in Ben Jonson's *Masque of Queens*; in the portrait, she appears to wear items of her Inigo Jones-designed costume from the masque (Arshad, 2019, pp. 105–44).[35] Daniel was Clifford's tutor.

Daniel's *Cleopatra* and its accompanying portrait bear witness to two kinds of theatrical deviship: Mary Sidney's, in commissioning Daniel to write *Cleopatra* as a sequel to her *Tragedie of Antonie* (translated from Robert Garnier's *Antoine*); and Anne Clifford's, in, as Arshad puts it '*playing* Cleopatra' (2019, p. 137) for the purposes of the portrait, and perhaps, in a costumed household performance. The activity detailed below invites students to perform a scene from *Cleopatra*, which Arshad, Helen Hackett, and I staged in a practice-as-research production at Goodenough College in 2013 (Figure 2), in a research project originated and led by Arshad. This activity was developed with Arshad and Hackett as part of this project; readers who wish to know more about Lady Anne Clifford and female household performance could consult our co-authored article (Arshad, Hackett, and Whipday, 2014).[36] Dorothy Heather Bowles' 2020 edition of the play (1601a) is freely available online.[37]

---

[35] This book grew from Arshad's PhD research.

[36] Thanks are due to the UCL Academy A Level students and the UCL Early Modern Studies MA students who experimented with this activity; this scene was also staged at the Shakespeare Institute and at Knole House for the National Trust, and I am grateful to both audiences for their insights.

[37] The extract in Appendix 2 is from the 1607 edition, available in Daniel, 1611a (with modernised spelling), which formed the basis of the 2013 production, while the copytext for Bowles' edition is Daniel, 1601b.

Figure 2 Charlotte Gallagher as Cleopatra and Charlotte Evans as Selecus in *The Tragedie of Cleopatra* directed by Emma Whipday, produced by Yasmin Arshad, and executive produced by Helen Hackett (2013), Goodenough College © Anna Wilton

---

☺ Activity 5: Implied Stage Directions

The principles of this activity can be applied to female-authored closet drama, or indeed, any scene in which there are 'implied stage directions': these are stage directions that are not explicit, separated from the dialogue and italicised, but implicit through references to embodied action in the speeches of the characters ('come', 'go', 'stay', 'here at thy conquering feet I lie'). Act III scene ii of Samuel Daniel's *The Tragedie of Cleopatra* (Appendix 2) is a particularly apt example because it contains a number of implied stage directions that are central to the meaning-making of the scene (Arshad, 2019, pp. 167–9).

Objectives

This activity will enable students to:

(1) find 'implied stage directions', in which characters' speech contains instructions for an embodied performance
(2) understand that these instructions can offer actors choice, opening up different possible readings of embodiment in the scene
(3) analyse how the interpretation of these clues affects the power dynamics of the scene, in relation to gender and status
(4) explore the significance of these embodied performance choices for a female performer in early modern England

Instructions

Students should read the scene (preferably aloud) in advance of staging it. This activity requires four volunteer students to perform the scene, with the rest of the group functioning as 'directors'. (Alternatively, students can perform it in small groups, and make directorial decisions themselves.) Students are instructed to pause in their performance every time an implied stage direction requires that a decision be made; at this point, the offstage 'directors' can make suggestions, and the group as a whole can discuss the implications of their choices.

The first implied stage direction occurs in Caesar's opening lines:

> What Cleopatra, dost thou doubt so much
> Of Caesar's mercy, that thou hid'st thy face?

This tells us that, at Caesar's entrance, Cleopatra's face is not visible to Caesar. Students must decide if she turns away in an impolite gesture, or hides her face with her hands while weeping (or pretending to), or does something else. Making such decisions requires students to reflect on the power dynamics in the scene: is Cleopatra emphasising her status as queen (in refusing to greet her unwelcome guests), or using Caesar's expectations of feminine behaviour (such as weeping) to attempt to manipulate him, or genuinely distraught?

The next significant implied stage direction is when Cleopatra tells Caesar: 'Yet now here at thy conquering feet I lie'. Caesar soon instructs her, 'Rise madame, rise', suggesting that Cleopatra literally lies at Caesar's feet. Again, there are embodied choices to be made: does Cleopatra prostrate herself, face first, in a posture of hyperbolic submission? Or does she lie on her back in a position that is at once mock-submissive, insolent, and suggestive?

Cleopatra then invites Caesar to read what appears to be a letter from her former lover, Julius Caesar ('these lines which still I keep with me'), which are presumably concealed somewhere about her person,[38] before drawing Caesar's attention to the (past) potential for a sexual relationship between them:

> For look what I have been to Antony,
> Think thou the same I might have been to thee.

There is no reply to this by Caesar; Cleopatra immediately moves to present Caesar with the list of her treasure. Students might decide here to leave a pause in which Caesar can react, silently, to the sexual provocation, with discomfort, dismissal, or disgust. The rest of the scene shows that Dolabella clearly reacts differently to Cleopatra's overtures, overcome by this 'charming beauty'; students might decide to demonstrate this in his silent reactions, which contrast with Caesar's.

Cleopatra's shift to presenting Caesar with a second document – the 'note' of all her 'treasure' – is another implied stage direction. Students can decide whether Cleopatra hands the note directly to Caesar or gestures to Selecus, to hand it over by proxy. Then, Selecus' betrayal prompts the one moment in the scene where two bodies touch, or almost touch – Cleopatra cries: 'What? vile and [un]grateful wretch . . . ', and Caesar responds, 'Hold, hold, a poor revenge, can work so feeble hands',

---

[38] These lines were cut from the 2013 production.

suggesting that Cleopatra's lines are coupled with some attempt at a violent action. Does Cleopatra succeed in striking Selecus before Caesar intervenes? Does Caesar stop her with words only, or do he and/or Dolabella restrain her? These decisions can then shape how Cleopatra plays her humiliated exit at the end of the scene.

This whole-group staging can then inform a whole-group discussion about the centrality of embodiment to the power dynamics in this scene. As Arshad, Hackett, and I argue in our article,

> Embodiment accentuated the dynamics of the play: this confrontation between Cleopatra and Caesar was fraught with a tense combination of mutual fascination and disgust, and invoked the sexual politics of Cleopatra's previous relations with Rome. (2014, p. 179)

Students can be invited to watch the performance of this scene in the recording of the Goodenough College production, and to compare the actors' choices with their own (see Appendix 4: Daniel, 2013, 51:42–1:01:00). In this production, Charlotte Gallagher, as Cleopatra, hides her face by turning away from Caesar (Beth Eyre) and Dollabella (Anna Sowerbutts); she then lies provocatively on the floor, emphasising the power she holds even as she places herself at Caesar's feet, and both Dolabella and Caesar must restrain her from striking Selecus (Charlotte Evans). This production was inspired by Anne Clifford's possible household performance; the majority of the cast are female, costumed in Jacobean-style clothing, and using period-appropriate gestures. This production can therefore inform a discussion on the significance of the possibility for female performance in relation to this play. How might an early modern noblewoman experience performing a role like that of Cleopatra, whether in a private reading, a fully staged household performance, or in portrait?

Follow-Up Activity: Performing the Chorus

Choruses in closet drama, which offer moralistic commentary, are likely to be particularly alien to a student reader. Inviting students to voice the Chorus by reading extracts aloud, and asking students to explore what the Chorus' objectives might be and how a (group) Chorus might be performed, can offer a way to interrogate the value systems each Chorus promotes. In Lady Jane Lumley's adaptation of Euripides' *The Tragedie of Iphigenia*, the Chorus has an explicit identity – the women of Aulis – who comments on the unfolding action in asides. Students can experiment with staging the Chorus, in, for example, the scene where the Chorus silently greets Clytemnestra and Iphigenia, simultaneously part of the play world and commentators on it. I suggest supplementing this activity by watching one of the recent stagings of Iphigenia – the Rose Company's full production,[39] or the University of Auckland's staged reading (Lumley, 2020). This Chorus can then be compared to the moralistic Chorus in Lady Elizabeth Cary's *The Tragedy of Mariam*; students can discuss the interpretations in Elizabeth Schafer's production, in which the Chorus is figured as Elizabeth Cary herself. Schafer has this Chorus read some of her lines aloud from a book, suggesting she voices conventional morality rather than her own opinions (Cary, 1995).

Witch Trial Accounts

The previous activities focused exclusively on elite performance and authorship. But how might students explore non-elite voices and performances? The next activity offers a very specific lens: that of printed witch trial narratives. Students are invited to voice the many competing voices in these texts – the (male) narrator, the interrogators, the witnesses, and the woman accused of witchcraft herself – as a way of close reading narrative voice, and of accessing the voices and creativities of the often illiterate women preserved in these accounts.

[39] See The Rose Company to purchase the DVD.

📖 What Is a Witch Trial Account?

Printed witch trial accounts offer what claims to be an accurate record of the activities of an accused and condemned witch. These texts come in a diverse range of forms: records of private interrogations of women accused of witchcraft by men in authority; trial documents involving witness statements by 'victims' and confessions by the accused women; and third-person narratives purporting to offer a 'true' account of the women's 'crimes'. What they all have in common is that they advertise themselves as providing access to 'truth', following the convention of early modern 'true crime' narratives, in the aftermath of the trial and execution of the accused women. Transcriptions of many of these accounts are freely available online (National Archives; Ray; Essex Witch Trials).[40]

Printed witch trial accounts offer a rich resource for the imaginative recovery of marginalised female voices and storytelling. They don't provide unmediated access to these voices: the women's stories were 'mediated by the men who wrote them down' (Gowing, 1996, p. 47), shaped by the questions asked, and by the cultural expectations of their stories. But we can nonetheless view these narratives as offering a mode of literary creation. Women who did not otherwise have access to authorship were pressured to confess according to preconceived expectations of witchcraft, but in confessing, they had the opportunity to create their own stories (albeit with fatal implications).

🎭 Activity 6: Voicing Witch Trials

This activity invites students to read witchcraft narratives 'against the grain'. These texts are crafted to warn their God-fearing readers of the destructive potential of witchcraft within the community, to prepare them to spot the signs of that witchcraft – and, of course, to

[40] See also Rosen, 1992; and Gibson, 2000, which include editions of the pamphlet in Appendix 3 Extract 3.

sensationalise, to entertain. Reading these texts in a form of imaginative recovery of female storytelling requires students to explore the relationship between the words of the women (as recorded in these texts) and the framing of their words in relation to the agendas of the male authority figures shaping these texts. Close reading these texts enables students to scrutinise them as rhetorical performances – and to examine the ideological values underpinning the language, voices, and narrative structure. Embodiment can also assist students in exploring the strange, uncanny, and dreamlike nature of many of these texts, which often encourage a departure from 'rational' modes of thought (Whipday, 2019b; Figure 3). Students should be encouraged to be alert to the gendered and classed power dynamics that limit these women's agency and expression, while engaging with their creativity in fashioning narratives of their own agency and dangerous power.

Figure 3 Maryam Grace, Joe Eyre, and Beth Eyre in a performance of an early modern witchcraft account directed by Asia Osborne, 'Witches at Night', Northern Stage, 2019 © Simon Veit-Wilson

Objectives

This activity will enable students to:

(1) understand the generic conventions of early modern printed witch trial accounts
(2) identify the different 'voices' in witch trial accounts
(3) make creative choices about how these voices can be performed
(4) analyse these records of 'real' voices as rhetorical performances that draw on legal and narrative conventions of storytelling about witchcraft

Instructions

This is an activity in two parts. The first centres on Henry Goodcole's *The Wonderfull Discoverie of Elizabeth Sawyer* (1621), a pamphlet which records Goodcole's prison visits to Sawyer, and his interrogation of her – and which would go on to form the source material for Dekker, Ford, and Rowley's 1621 tragicomedy, *The Witch of Edmonton*.[41] The pamphlet is structured as a dialogue granting us: Goodcole's questions; Sawyer's answers; Sawyer's memories of her own previous conversations with her demonic 'familiar' (a demon in animal form); and Goodcole's occasionally brutal marginal commentary:

Question

In what place of your body did the Devil suck of your blood, and whether did he himself choose the place, or did you your self appoint him the place? tell the truth, I charge you, as you will answer unto the Almighty God, and tell the reason if that you can, why he would suck your blood.

---

[41] See Dekker, Ford, and Rowley, 1621b. A modern spelling edition of the pamphlet is available in the Appendix to Dekker, Ford, and Rowley, 1621a, pp. 135–49.

[Marginal note: I demanded this question of her to confirm the women's search of her, concerning, that she had such a mark about her, which they upon their oaths informed the court, that truth it was, she had such a mark.]

Answer

The place where the Devil sucked my blood was a little above my fundiment, and that place chosen by himself; and in that place by continual drawing, there is a thing in the form of a Teat, at which the Devil would suck me. And I asked the Devil why he would suck my blood, and he said it was to nourish him.

Here, we can see that, in reproducing a dialogue, Goodcole's narrative makes explicit the relationship between the narrator's voice; the reported voices of the dialogue; and the speech reported by Sawyer within that dialogue.

Two volunteer students can be invited to read an extract aloud for the group (Appendix 3 Extract 1), with the rest of the group functioning as the audience. Alternatively, students can be split into small groups, and read aloud and make decisions together, before reporting back to the wider group. The audience can be invited to think about the extract as a performance text – both a record of an oral conversation between Goodcole and Sawyer, and a sensational text by Goodcole, designed to be read aloud. They are to listen to the distinction between the moments when Goodcole speaks to Sawyer, and the moments when he speaks to the reader directly; and to consider the extent to which Sawyer, in answering Goodcole, is shaping her own narrative of witchcraft, and the extent to which her story is shaped by the leading questions asked by Goodcole. Students might also want to consider how much agency Sawyer grants herself in her own telling, and how much she lays the responsibility for her actions on her demonic 'familiar'. Students can then reflect on how they feel in voicing or hearing this conversation from four hundred years ago, between the clergyman who visited condemned criminals to offer religious comfort and then sold their stories, and the woman accused of witchcraft, who will shortly hang for it.

In part II of the exercise, students can then be divided into small groups to engage with an unfamiliar extract. One possible extract is 'The examination of Joan Prentice', from *The Apprehension and Confession of Three Notorious Witches* (Anon, 1598) (Appendix 2 Extract 2). Students are placed in groups of three or four, and asked to read the extract, to discuss its features of interest, and to find a way to voice or stage its account of a woman selling her soul to the devil in the form of a ferret.

There are four possible voices in this extract: the third person narrator (the scribe), who describes Joan in legal terms as 'this examinate'; Joan Prentice, telling her story in answer to (unrecorded) questions, whose words have been converted by the scribe from first person to third person; the Joan in the story, speaking to her familiar; and the familiar himself, whose speech she records, as follows:

> the ferret standing with his hinderlegs upon the ground,
> and his forelegs settled upon her lap, and settling his fiery
> eyes upon her eyes, spake and pronounced to her these
> words following, namely: Joan Prentice give me thy
> soul, to whom this Examinate being greatly amazed,
> answered and said: In the name of God what art thou.

Students are invited to consider how they might stage the encounter between the 'witch' and her familiar, in relation to the witch's narration of this encounter. Does the scribe speak on Joan's behalf, narrating the account, while Joan speaks only in her reported speech in her own memory (e.g. 'In the name of God what art thou')? Or do they turn the third person pronouns ('this Examinate being greatly amazed') to first person ('I being greatly amazed'), so that Joan herself can speak it? Are past and present tense Joan voiced by the same person? Is the familiar voiced, or simply remembered by Joan? There is no 'right' answer – this could be a multi-vocal, fully staged performance, with a student as the scribe framing it with terms like 'the said Examinate saith', another student voicing Joan in the courtroom (converted to the first person), another voicing past tense Joan in her memory, another the familiar confronting her in her bedchamber (perhaps embodying the physicality of a ferret!) – or it could simply be read aloud entirely in the first person, as if by Joan in the courtroom, or in the third person, as if by the recording scribe repeating what he has recorded. Students might find it useful to highlight the text in different colours to make the different possibilities visible, when making this decision.

Volunteers can then demonstrate their performance choices to the group as a whole (or, if they prefer, describe how they would voice or perform the extract). Students can collaboratively close read the details of the text, thinking about which aspects of the text (the language; the imagery; the gender dynamics; the strangeness; the legal emphasis on time, place, and evidence) their staging highlighted. This activity gives students the opportunity to explore: the language and narrative features of the text; what message the author is trying to convey, and how this relates to their beliefs; and the power dynamics between the woman confessing witchcraft and those representing and framing her words. It can raise questions about who gets to speak, and in what context, and how agency is demonstrated (or diminished) through speech. It can also open up a wider discussion of the possibilities and difficulties inherent in attempting to recover female voices.

Follow-Up Activity: Staging a Witch Trial

After exploring how to perform a witch trial account in a classroom context, students can work collaboratively to stage an entire witch trial. *A True and Juste Recorde* (Anon, 1582) contains a wide range of depositions by 'witnesses', 'victims', and women accused of witchcraft (Appendix 3 Extract 3).[42] Each small group of students can be given

---

[42] This activity was developed when co-teaching these extracts with Ruth Connolly on the 'Renaissance Bodies' module; Ruth also co-edited Appendix 3 Extract 3. I am grateful to Ruth for her insights. Staging this witch trial can enable students to create historic 'verbatim theatre'; see Munro and Whipday, 2020.

a different deposition or confession from the same trial to prepare in advance of the seminar. Volunteer students then voice or stage their extract for the rest of the group, and all students can share what they have learned about the voices, narrative structure, and power dynamics of their extract, in the process of preparing these texts for performance. In exploring how 'their' extract can be voiced, students can gain a sense of ownership of this particular extract, and 'learn by teaching' by sharing their findings with the group as a whole (in a variation on the 'flipped classroom').[43]

Many scholars have commented on how working with archival materials in the classroom can 'give students the experience of doing "real research"' (Blackstone, 2006, p. 44), and enable them to 'take responsibility for their own learning by giving them the authority in the classroom to do so' (Donaweth, 1996, p. 476). Ann Hurley (2000) suggests that encouraging students to find primary materials themselves can further transform the power structures of the classroom: 'they are not handed authority; they generate it themselves' (p. 255), so that 'a group of individuals who had entered a classroom as students emerge from it as genuine scholars' (p. 257). These statements imply that students' 'authority' and status as 'genuine scholars' doing 'real research' comes from the students' knowledge of, and engagement with, difficult-to-access archival materials – engaging with these marginalised materials grants students access to specialist knowledge, and therefore enables them to access the status of 'specialist'.

I suggest the above activities can grant students a different form of authority in the classroom, and enable them to inhabit a different model of scholarship. The activities suggested above do indeed enable students engage with non-canonical, difficult-to-access, and, in some cases, non-literary texts. But I suggest that in the aforementioned activities, students' authority stems not (or not only) from the fact *that* they engage with these texts, but rather, in *how* they engage with these texts; in their ability to close read these texts in relation to questions of gender, power, and performance. This close reading is

---

[43] See Bargh and Schul, 1980; and Strayer, 2012.

informed by embodied, voiced, and creative approaches to these texts; and these activities aim to enable students to create their own informed interpretations of these texts, rooted in textual evidence, and contributing to a wider understanding of the role of female voices, performances, and experiences in early modern culture. Performing these scenes can offer students a form of creative authority: students are making creative choices about textual details that can at once inform their readings of these texts, and put their own creativity in conversation with that of early modern women. In making performance choices – about how to express a literary image through a tableaux, about how to identify and interpret implicit stage directions, about how to voice and perform the complex narrative strategies of witch trial accounts – students claim ownership of their own reading and interpretation of these texts. Furthermore, the cumulative effect of the exercises in this section enables students to gain a nuanced awareness of both the diversity of forms of early modern performance, and the complexities of gendered power dynamics in (and produced by) early modern culture.

In the 1996 special issue of *Shakespeare Quarterly* on 'Teaching Judith Shakespeare', Nancy Gutierrez argues that, in her experience, including a single female-authored text (such as *Mariam*) on a Shakespeare-focused course forces that play to assume an outsized importance:

> *The Tragedy of Mariam* stood for writing by female contemporaries of Shakespeare ... [W]orks were judged according to their 'artistic' merits, and the woman's text was deemed inferior. (p. 427)

In offering a wider range of writing, voicing, and performance by the female contemporaries of Shakespeare, we can avoid asking a single work by a single female author to 'stand in' for all early modern female authorship and be weighed against Shakespeare. Furthermore, in giving a sense of the broad range of contexts in which female deviband operated, we can give students the opportunity to situate Shakespeare's plays as just one vibrant part of the rich, multifaceted, and complex landscape of early modern performance culture. The above exercises enable students to access that world; to experience the voices and performances of women as 'live'; to re-make the canon; to gain creative authority through engaging with unfamiliar texts; to explore the complexities of gender and power in early modern culture; and to use embodiment and creativity to close read these texts.

3 Teaching Embodiment Online

This Element has so far explored the possibilities for enactive, kinaesthetic, creative, embodied learning, suggesting that teachers can enhance their students' learning by using bodies and voices as frameworks for close readings of texts and histories. The first two sections have focused exclusively on in-person teaching exercises, which rely on the co-presence of teacher and students. However, this Element was written in 2021–22, in the immediate aftermath of an academic year in which repeated lockdowns necessitated an international shift to online (or, in some cases, 'blended' or 'hybrid') university teaching. I, like many of my colleagues, had to create, at short notice, digital alternatives to the embodied pedagogies central to my teaching of Shakespeare and his sisters. I therefore taught 'Women on Trial' – the third-year, specialist module in which I developed many of the activities in previous sections – online-only, through pre-recorded lectures, asynchronous learning materials and exercises, synchronous watch parties, and seminars and performance workshops via group video call.[44] This final section offers versions of the activities in the previous sections adapted for

---

[44] In this section, I draw on the students' mid-module and end-of-module feedback, via two online questionnaires. The mid-module questionnaire asked students four questions: (1) What have you enjoyed about this module so far? (2) What is one new thing you have learned on this module so far? (3) How helpful have you found creative learning methods – performance workshops, 'wild card' activities, and collaborative close reading – in developing your thinking about module texts? (4) What is one thing you would like me to know about your experience of this module? (This could be something you haven't understood, something you think could be changed or improved, or something you'd like to see more of.) The end-of-module questionnaire asked students only one question: 'Is there anything you'd like me to know about your experience of the module – anything you particularly enjoyed, or anything you would like to see changed?' I am very grateful to students quoted here for permitting me to share their responses.

online learning environments alongside new, online-only activities, and reflects on ways that students' embodied learning can be facilitated without the co-presence of bodies and voices in a shared physical space.

Students today are particularly well placed to engage with such experiments. As Peter Kirwan observed in 2014:

> The students who are now entering higher education are the Web 2.0 Generation, used to a read-and-write internet, and to producing content as well as absorbing it ... [S]tudents increasingly expect to be *doing*. (2014a, p. 101)

The same is doubly true at the time this Element goes to press, reinforced by over a year of digital pedagogies and 'blended learning' necessitated by Covid-19 and the 2020–21 lockdowns. The following exercises are enactive, designed for students accustomed to a read-and-write internet; they enable students both to learn by doing and to participate in an online learning community facilitated by what Erin Sullivan describes as the interpersonal, 'adaptable, reflexive, immediate, and personal' nature of online communication (2014, p. 72).

In this section, where I use an example from a playhouse play, I choose, not a play by Shakespeare, but a play by one of his (male) contemporaries. A fuller exploration of ways of teaching Shakespeare's playhouse contemporaries alongside the plays of Shakespeare and his sisters is outside the scope of this Element;[45] however, it is a key part of the pedagogy of the 'Women on Trial' module on which this section reflects, and I therefore gesture towards the possibilities for doing this in my examples. Some of the activities in earlier sections can be easily adapted to an online context. The movement aspect of 'Activity 1: Playing with Bodies' can be recreated by students in whatever space they find themselves, with cameras on or off depending on comfort levels, though the social aspects can only be imagined. 'Activity 6: Voicing Witch Trials', as a small-group activity in voicing and performing non-literary texts, can be managed by dividing students on a video call into break-out groups (or inviting students to work

---

[45] I recommend Hiscock and Hopkins, 2007.

together to prepare presentations in advance), after which they can present their texts for the whole group. I have focused below on activities that require more adjustment, and on online-only exercises that aim to offer key elements of the in-person classroom, namely social interaction (Kumpulainen and Wray, 2002), peer-to-peer learning (Tullis and Goldstone, 2020), and attention to liveness in performance (Kirwan, 2014b).

As noted above, this section was inspired by an enforced online 'pivot'; it therefore represents an attempt to replicate the outcomes of embodied teaching online through necessity, rather than as a considered transition. But the success of these methods surprised me; while much of my teaching is now in-person (and, as in many educational contexts, there are political and economic, as well as pedagogical, reasons for this), I have retained many of the activities below in my post-lockdown teaching, in a form of 'blended' learning that informs and supplements my in-person seminars, lectures, and workshops. I therefore reproduce them here, not as a last resort for those occasions that necessitate an online pivot, but as digital methods that can supplement in-person embodied learning, and can also offer gains specific to working digitally. In this section, I suggest that online activities can offer opportunities for creativity, collaboration, peer-to-peer learning, and social engagement that equal or exceed those of in-person teaching; can be a welcoming space for less confident students who might not speak in a physical seminar room but might share their thoughts online; and can, perhaps surprisingly, enable modes of close reading that are particularly alert to the embodied potential of performance texts.

🎭 Activity 7: Role-Playing Online

A common rehearsal room technique is that of role-playing: improvising in character.[46] Role-playing offers an immediate, personal, emotive way for students to access the more abstract concerns of early modern texts in the classroom. This activity enables an entire cohort of students to experience role-playing, and to respond to each other, online,

---

[46] This activity resembles 'hot-seating' (Gibson, 1998, p. 98).

through the conceit of the Reddit thread 'Am I The Asshole?' This thread is a crowd-sourced problem page: anonymous users post their problems, usually a moral dilemma relating to a relationship (be it romantic, sexual, familial, friendship, or workplace), and ask whether they are 'the asshole' in the situation described. Readers then comment with their own opinions on the situation, in an example of what Kirwan termed the 'read-and-write internet'. In applying the AITA conceit to the characters from an early modern play, students are able to probe the ways in which a play positions the moral dilemmas of its characters in relation to its wider moral universe, and how this speaks to the concerns of early modern society more broadly.

Objectives

This activity will enable students to:

(1) identify a moral dilemma, or morally complex situation, experienced in an early modern play
(2) comprehend the ideological underpinnings of this moral dilemma, in relation to the world of the play
(3) explore, from a first-person perspective, how a particular character experiences this moral dilemma
(4) support this exploration with appropriate textual evidence
(5) respond to, and learn from, the responses of peers
(6) reflect on how the play itself presents this moral dilemma, and whether it encourages the audience to 'side' with a particular perspective

Instructions

This task requires some form of message board on which students can post or comment; this can be hosted on a Virtual Learning Environment (VLE), but I chose the publicly available message board website Padlet, as it enables students easily to comment on and 'like' each other's posts, creating a sense of a social online community. Each student posts as their character, outlining a moral dilemma (or morally complex situation) in which they are involved, asking if they are the 'asshole' in that situation. Students should post in their own words, but should also include at least one supporting quotation from the play itself (to encourage students to use textual evidence to support their argument). More than one student can post as the same character; any differences in approach will be instructive in the following discussion.

After posting their own dilemma, students should then comment on the posts of at least two other characters. They can do so as their character (in which case, they should sign the name of their character at the end of the post), or as themselves. For example, in the anonymous 1592 domestic tragedy *Arden of Faversham*, Susan might post that her mistress is asking her to help cover up the murder of her master – and ask if she is the asshole in agreeing to do it, considering that she 'knew not of it til the deed was done' (Anon, 1592, 18.19–20). In response, another student might post as Michael, blaming Susan for being offered by her mistress as a reward for his participation in the murder; and another student might post as themselves, pointing out Susan's subordinate gender, class, and household position and consequent vulnerability to manipulation. Students should read each other's posts and comments in advance of a synchronous group discussion (on a video call for an online-only module, or 'in person' in a seminar for a 'blended' module).

In the group discussion, students can be asked how they defended their character's position in the AITA post – how did they explain their moral dilemma or ambiguous situation? Did they defend their behaviour according to particular values or codes of behaviour, or did two or more ideologies clash in their dilemma? For example, Susan might say that she was obedient to both her mistress and her brother in covering up their murder of her master, and in so doing, she acted according to the hierarchical ideology of the early modern household, but this clashed with other ideologies, such as the law, and Christianity (Whipday, 2019a, pp. 77–82). This can open up a wider discussion about the value systems of the play.

This activity, in encouraging students to experience the world of the play from the perspective of a particular character, enables students to develop the building-blocks of literary scholarship – supporting observations with textual examples; situating these examples in relation to the concerns of the play; exploring how a play engages with wider social, moral, and political concerns; constructing an argument – in a way that feels more relaxed and playful, and with lower stakes, than traditional academic discourse. It also enables students to engage with the ideological work a play performs through a precise and specific reading, in a way that might not be possible in a more generalised seminar discussion. English Literature students may find a creative exercise like this unexpected; it can be helpful to frame it in a way that makes clear its utility, perhaps by highlighting how it will be built on in seminar discussions to open up larger literary, theatrical, moral, and historical questions.

The students in my 2020–21 cohort commented on how 'fun' and 'entertaining' they found this activity (with one noting that AITA comments and responses 'don't feel like work, so you are more likely to work on them in your own time' – indeed, the idea of the activities in this section 'not feeling like work' cropped up more than once in the module feedback). Students also noted, in impressively self-aware reflections on their own learning processes, how this activity informed their readings of the module plays:

> [The activity] allowed me to really step into the mind of the character (or characters) I chose and understand their motives and mindset, rather than looking at them at face value, which ultimately improved my understanding and bettered my sense of analysis and mode of thought about the texts.

As one student put it, this activity was 'helpful for expanding my critical thinking in a creative way', giving rise to 'original' insights. Another student commented that 'the exercise allowed me to understand the characters more and by responding to other posts/seeing other peers respond, seeing things they have noticed, which I may have skimmed over': peer-to-peer learning was a key element of this students' engagement with the module, and most students appreciated the possibilities for social engagement and collaborative learning in an informal learning community, in a context in which informal interaction with their peers was severely limited. Thompson and Turchi observe that informal learning communities in a Shakespeare classroom can offer students 'opportunities to make meaning together, combining their insights and pooling their understanding' (2016, p. 4); the opportunity, in this activity, to choose one of a range of characters enables students working on the same character to combine their insights, while learning from those who chose a different character, producing a cumulative understanding of the moral world of the play. Peer-to-peer learning is often discussed in relation to the 'mastery' of material students develop in teaching their peers (Awan, 2021), but in this case, students are not aiming to 'teach' through completing these activities; rather, they develop what Jean Lave and Etienne Wenger have termed a 'community of practice' through repeated interactions (in their posts and comments) to create a shared repertoire of creative close readings while building 'meaningful social relationships'.[47] This community of practice enables students to build on each other's insights in a form of collaborative, creative close reading that can, as the students above note, inform a wider understanding of the play, preparing students for traditional modes of assessment (such as the essay).

This 'community of practice' can also be developed 'live', through synchronous online teaching. However, in an online classroom, embodied in-person performance of scenes, such as Activity 3: 'Staging the Scene' and Activity 5: 'Implied Stage Directions', is not possible. For English Literature students unused to attending to cues for performance, it can be difficult to develop the facility to identify and analyse these in the absence of such activities (even if modelled by a lecturer and informed by the insights of peers). As Kirwan notes, 'the question remains of how students can be encouraged to embrace the live, particularly when treating subject matter that is dependent on an

---

[47] Lave and Wenger, 1991; Wenger, 1991.

understanding of live performance' (2014b, p. 60). I suggest that 'watch parties' and online performance workshops offer two different, but complementary, ways of exploring the liveness of performance with students, even in the absence of embodied, performance-based exercises. Combining these kinds of exercises with the role-playing described above can enable students to approach text-based analysis with a clearer framework for noting performance-related features of a text.

⧉ Activity 8: Watch Parties

When staging scenes in the classroom isn't possible (and live performances of plays may be equally inaccessible), recordings of existing productions can both enable students to engage with actors' and directors' specific performance choices, and help students to identify the moments of choice, working against a tendency to engage with literary texts as fixed and static. There are, of course, countless online versions of productions of Shakespeare plays available, via (among others) Shakespeare's Globe's Globe Player platform, Bloomsbury's Drama Online platform (which features a rich range of productions, from the RSC, the National Theatre, and Shakespeare's Globe, among others), Box of Broadcasts (BoB, for accessing any productions previously streamed on UK television, such as BBC Shakespeare), and MIT's Global Shakespeares Video and Performance Archive. Productions of masques and closet dramas are more difficult to access, but, as the previous section has demonstrated, not impossible. Students can of course be encouraged to access these productions in their own time. The benefits of a watch party include the fact that it can foster a sense of 'liveness' even when engaging with a recorded performance, through the creation of a virtual, synchronous 'audience', as well as enabling a form of live, collaborative close reading of performance choices.[48]

---

[48] I am grateful to my colleagues on 'Renaissance Bodies' – Ruth Connolly, Jennifer Richards, Kate De Rycker, and Rachel White – for experimenting with this format with me.

Objectives

This activity will enable students to:

(1) identify moments where the performers and directors have made choices in response to textual cues
(2) respond to the overall 'vision' for the production, in relation to staging, design, and sound choices
(3) share opinions about the success of these choices
(4) build on peers' observations and opinions
(5) note any areas of difficulty, and ask questions in response

Instructions

A 'watch party' involves simultaneous watching of a recorded (or streamed) production, combined with a live text chat between teacher and students. In the pandemic, many university teachers have explored the possibilities for lecture watch parties, as a form of 'flipped classroom' (Compton, 2020; MacNeill, 2021), while shared online communities have formed (via Twitter and other platforms) to experience a version of 'live' theatre together. The text chat itself can take place on any platform (with a low bandwidth, if possible, to enable students with poor internet connections to stream simultaneously); Discord is a popular choice, while the majority of VLEs have some kind of 'chat' option. Students can be encouraged, where possible, to use a second device (such as a phone) for the 'chat', to enable them to watch the production without navigating away from the screen.

The chat can begin with students being invited to comment on specific elements of a production, as they crop up (e.g. gesture; the sense of place; the use of props; character relationships). However, in my experience, students' own experiences of informal, social watch parties can inform how they engage with the chat, creating a free-flowing discussion far beyond the parameters set up by the initial instructions. Students can be encouraged to comment on anything they find of interest, and also to ask questions, both about anything that puzzles them and about how particular production choices link to wider concerns of the course.

If an in-person screening is possible, the 'watch party' framework can still be used, with students invited to chat on their devices while watching via a communal screen. This can offer a more social experience than simply attending a screening in silence, and can enable a more detailed discussion than would be possible at the end of a lengthy screening. Students can be invited to offer informal, emotional reactions (surprise, laughter, horror) in a way that can supplement the laughter or gasps that are often expressed at a theatre or cinema, but can be stifled in a lecture hall; the combination of digital chat and physical co-presence can double the students' experience of becoming a live audience, even when the production itself is no longer 'live'.

However, one thing to keep in mind if using online chat functions in an in-person screening is that students may be less comfortable participating in an online chat when they can see the other participants in a shared space; those students who are less confident participating in in-person seminar discussions may feel a similar discomfort when the other 'chatters' are visible to them, a discomfort that can be alleviated by the relative invisibility of an online-only text conversation. In my (admittedly anecdotal) experience I have found this to be particularly the case when students are accustomed to online watch parties, and then attend an in-person watch party with an online chat element; in this case the existing sense of an informal online community was not strengthened, but rather weakened, by the students' co-presence, and few students could be persuaded to participate in the text conversation. Online-only watch parties also have the benefit of mimicking the conditions of social watch parties with which they might be familiar from lockdown, and therefore make a free-flowing, informal conversation the more likely.

🎭 Activity 9: Performance Workshops

A screening can enable students to respond to the staging choices of others; a performance workshop can enable students to make their own. Like the exercise above, this whole-group exercise can complement small-group, text-based exercises (e.g. Activity 6: Voicing Witch Trials), informing how students will approach a close reading of a performance text.

Objectives

This exercise will enable students to:

(1) identify explicit and implied stage directions, in which cues for performance are provided by the playtext
(2) understand that these cues can offer actors choice, opening up different possible readings of embodiment, speech and silence, and stage properties in the scene
(3) analyse how the interpretation of these cues affects our understanding of characterisation, power dynamics, and complicity
(4) share real-time written responses to the performance cues in an informal, low-pressure environment
(5) respond to, and learn from, the responses of peers

Instructions

A performance workshop online is very similar to a performance workshop in-person: the same questions can be asked of the scene, the same words can be voiced. Activities 3 ('Staging the Scene') and 5 ('Implied Stage Directions') can function as a whole-group exercise online. But there is one key difference: in an online workshop, the interaction of bodies, voices, and space is entirely imagined. Constant attention to the embodied potential of the scene is required, particularly if students are more accustomed to literary close reading.

This exercise requires a video calling platform with a 'chat' function (it was developed on Zoom, but can be used on any comparable platform). Students are given a scene or extract, from a play which they have already read in its entirety; for example, students studying Webster's *The White Devil* might be given the dumb show:

CONJURER: Pray sit down,
Put on this night-cap sir, 'tis charmed, and now
I'll show you by my strong-commanding art
The circumstances that breaks your Duchess' heart.

A DUMB SHOW

Enter suspiciously DOCTOR JULIO and CRISTOFERO. They draw a curtain where BRACHIANO's picture is; they put on spectacles of glass which cover their eyes and noses, and then burn perfumes afore the picture and wash the lips of the picture. That done, quenching the fire, and putting off their spectacles, they depart laughing. Enter ISABELLA in her nightgown as to bedward, with lights after her, Count LODOVICO, GIOVANNI, GUID-ANTONIO and others waiting on her. She kneels down as to prayers, then draws the curtain of the picture, does three reverences to it and kisses it thrice. She faints and will not suffer them to come near it; dies. Sorrow expressed in GIOVANNI and in Count LODOVICO. She's conveyed out solemnly.

BRACHIANO: Excellent; then she's dead ... (Webster, 1612, II. ii.21–31)

Three student volunteers can be invited to read aloud – as the Conjuror, Brachiano, and the voice of the stage directions. The rest of the students can be invited to think about the relationship between the speech and the spectacle, and what the staging choices in the dumb show communicate (particularly use of costumes and properties, gesture, descriptions of move-ment, interactions between bodies, etc.). They are invited to type in the chat any thoughts that occur to them during the dumb show and afterwards. It may be helpful to suggest that students treat the comments box as a form of note-taking: rather than only commenting when they have a profound insight (which can often lead to self-consciousness), it is an expectation that everyone will comment more than once in the course of the workshop, so there is no weight placed on any one particular comment. Rather, the teacher is looking at the cumulative effect of the comments – which features do several students comment upon? What goes unnoticed? Do interpretations of the same features differ?

This can lead to a much wider (and more numerous) range of responses than a traditional seminar or performance workshop discussion. The degree of intervention and commenting by the teacher that this format necessitates can be helpful in ensuring students are continually reminded to focus on the performance-related, as well as the literary, features of the scene. It can be helpful if this is framed in relation to the lost opportunities for staging that the virtual workshop won't allow; for example, in an in-person workshop student volunteers would stage the silent roles of Doctor Julio, Cristofero, Isabella, Count Lodovico, Giovanni, and Guid-Antonio (and perhaps also Brachiano's portrait). In the absence of volunteers embodying these parts, some students might be willing to volunteer as silent participants, invited to imagine the choices they would make and the ways they would move in performance, and to comment on these in the chat.

Questions might include: what does it mean to 'enter suspiciously'? What effect would burning perfumes onstage produce? What is the significance of Isabella being dressed in her nightgown? How might the direction 'she kneels down as to prayers' encourage the audience to view this scene? What might her reverences look like, and where might she kiss the portrait? How might her faint be performed, considering that she must 'not suffer them to come near it' as she does so? How might her death be performed? How might Giovanni and Lodovico express sorrow? The 'silent' volunteers can be invited to respond to these kinds of questions in the chat, from the perspective of their particular character – and the 'audience' students can also comment on anything they notice. Brachiano and the Conjuror can be invited to comment on their own words, but might also want to consider their own silences – their role as onstage observers to the dumb show action. The teacher can offer their own response to what students have noticed (and not noticed) in the comments, by first reading aloud student responses and then commenting on those responses, before opening up a wider discussion with students (by text or on mic) about the relationship between the dumb show and the rest of the play's action, and how the audience (like Brachiano) becomes complicit in watching the dumb show murders. They might also discuss whether Isabella, in idolising her husband enough to kneel before his portrait 'as if at prayer' (and kiss and curtsey), is behaving as a hyperbolic, idealised early modern wife, or if she is being portrayed as a Catholic idolater who takes her love for her husband too far (Woods, 2017).

A virtual performance workshop requires a greater imaginative effort on the part of the students than a physical workshop, but it can be rewarding. One student commented:

> I also like the group analysis etc in the performance workshop as it's really interesting and insightful to get everyone's opinions and thoughts on, for example the scene we are looking at. Especially if I haven't understood the text as much this week or not been sure on what my thoughts are, I've found the thoughts and analysis by the lecturer and my peers particularly helpful.

Another noted:

> The performance workshops have been really helpful for discussing ideas and reading collectively, almost as if it's an opportunity to know how the play would be performed in a way.

As with previous exercises, students relished the opportunity to learn from their peers; they also, as in the second comment, explicitly recognised the benefits of thinking through performance, even when embodied performance was impossible.

Yet, unlike the watch parties, which received universally positive feed-back (both during the online-only year and during the subsequent, 'blended' year), the performance workshops proved the most divisive element of this module; in mid-module feedback, one student commented that they found 'the reading aloud not as helpful' but did 'find it very useful the part where there are questions posed about what we've read and we put in the group chat our thoughts', while another noted that 'my focus wavers around the 90-minute mark', and a third observed, 'I don't see the point in listening to people reading out a play that I have already read'. Students' challenges with sustaining focus, and with comprehending the value of the tasks, were in part due to the initial format of the performance workshops, something I adapted over the course of the module. Having enjoyed Zoom playreadings myself as a precious form of live performance in lockdown (Myles), I initially aimed to make performance workshops as close to a playreading as possible; while there wasn't time to read a play in its entirety, I invited students to read lengthy scenes aloud, pausing only every several pages – in one notable case, reading and discussing the long opening scene of *Arden of Faversham* took the majority of the two-hour session. After receiving the above feedback, I altered the format so that the online performance workshops, like those in person, concentrated in great detail on a single scene (or perhaps two), pausing every few lines to engage with the comments in the chat and to develop our readings further. I also encouraged students to engage in meta-cognition, reflecting on the early modern culture of reading aloud, and on how voicing texts can offer a mode of reading them, by sharing Jennifer Richards' argument that early modern writers 'often assume that their work will or could be read aloud and imagine the effects of the voice on interpretation in ways we have been slow to notice' (2019, p. 25). The act of reading aloud became especially significant when reading texts such as church court records and trial accounts, where reading aloud meant recreating 'real' voices from the past.

Despite the frustrations of some students earlier in the module, the performance workshops clearly had some effect. 'Women on Trial' was assessed in three ways: a 750-word close reading of an extract, chosen by the student, from a performance text (which could be a scene from a play for the professional stage, or one of the range of categories of performance texts mentioned in Section 2), for 20 per cent of the final mark; a 2,750-word essay, discussing a play for the professional stage (by Shakespeare or a male contemporary) in relation to another kind of performance text, for 70 per cent; and a 500-word reflection on the student's participation in and engagement with the module, for 10 per cent. I taught 'Women on Trial' for two years in person before teaching the online version of the course, and I was astonished to find of the online cohort, when marking the mid-module close readings and end-of-module essays, that almost all students engaged with the performance features of their chosen text in far greater detail (and with far greater success) than any previous cohort. The imaginative efforts involved in virtual performance workshops seem to have reaped greater rewards even than physical performance workshops. Of course, this evidence is partial and limited, based on a single cohort in extreme circumstances (and I must here note the laudable engagement shown by this cohort in such circumstances, as well as the extremely impressive work they produced). But I hope that these activities suggest one way that embodied learning can be used as fruitfully at a distance as it can in person.

This may perhaps invite the question, if students can successfully approach early modern drama through the lens of embodiment online, without participating in any of the embodied activities outlined in the previous sections, then what is the value of those activities? A student could theoretically successfully complete each of the activities in this section in an entirely text-based way: writing comments on AITA posts and commenting in the chat in the performance workshop and watch party. This hypothetical student could gain a rich understanding of the significance of performance, embodiment, and creativity as modes of reading early modern plays while using a more traditional text-based approach, rather than the movement- and voice-based exercises suggested in the earlier sections. If this is possible in the digital world, is it not equally possible in the classroom? Does this negate my emphasis on learning through moving bodies and speaking voices?

I suggest not. Or rather, I suggest that there is something specific to the digital modes of engagement I outline above that enables students to engage with embodiment in a disembodied way. Creating what Anna Hegland has termed a 'virtual rehearsal space' (Hegland, 2021, p. 15) requires an acknowledgement that participants are not sharing a space; that even 'synchronous' modes of online communication involve a slight delay in the cues, verbal and non-verbal, that make up communication; that voices are digitally relayed; that three-dimensional bodies are rendered two-dimensional, or represented only by the face, or not visible at all. Engaging together in any act of play-making or performance therefore requires an additional imaginative effort – perhaps not unlike the imaginative work we undertake, and early modern audiences undertook, at the theatre. We are simultaneously 'with' our online community, and spatially remote from them: there and not-there.

The effort involved in this imaginative work is conscious, as the many think pieces about Zoom fatigue attest (Sander and Bauman, 2020). When I ask students to read aloud a stage direction and to imagine it in performance, the task is not so very far removed from the work they are already doing in imagining the series of boxes on their Zoom screen as a learning community. As I have suggested above, this can, in my experience, encourage students to make the imaginative leap to thinking about a written text in performance – which students are then able to replicate when close reading a text alone, perhaps even more successfully than a student who has first experienced a collaborative close reading of a text in physical performance, and then must translate that skill to the page.

In my (partial and limited) experience, this kind of imaginative leap does not necessarily translate to the seminar room – or at least, not to the seminar rooms I experienced when teaching the second-year module 'Renaissance Bodies' in autumn 2021, with a masked cohort required to follow social distancing guidelines. Buoyed by the success of these online workshops, I attempted, in physical, in-person seminar rooms, to replicate their success, asking students to close read a scene in relation to performance *without* staging it (and therefore avoiding the forbidden proximity that staging might necessitate). But I found this surprisingly difficult; students were understandably resistant to imagining themselves performing, while aware of their physical, seated, unmoving co-presence. Their literary close readings were thoughtful and precise, but they were unwilling, or unable, to offer performance-based close reading. In contrast, returning to the embodied activities chronicled in previous sections with masked third-year students on the new module 'Gender, Power, and Performance in Early

Modern Culture' (co-designed and taught with Kate Chedgzoy) in spring 2022, without the social distancing requirement, was as successful as pre-pandemic experiments – perhaps more so, given many students' excitement about being able to engage in these kinds of activities in person.

This is not to suggest that it is impossible to replicate the success of these online activities in person. A student can experience an embodied, creative approach to Shakespeare (and his sisters) while typing at their laptop when surrounded by their peers in a classroom, as in a library or their bedroom – it simply requires an imaginative effort, and a framework within which these efforts can be understood. Establishing this framework in a physical seminar space can, paradoxically, be more difficult than establishing it in a synchronous, virtual 'space' online, where imagination is already a prerequisite.

What is valuable in each of these approaches – embodied and online – is how they invite us to attend to questions of embodiment, space, time, vocality, creativity, and performance. The texts on which this Element focuses – the plays of Shakespeare, his sisters, and, in this section, his brothers – record, prompt, and imagine embodied performance; whether in a multi-sensory purpose-built playhouse, or in a wider range of performance contexts, from the Court to the courtroom, and from country houses to prisons. These texts are rich in cues for, and traces of, embodiment – cues and traces that are all too easily lost to the silent reader, whether student or teacher. Bringing our own bodies, voices, and imaginations to these texts can help us to pay attention.

Conclusion

It feels fitting to end this Element with the comments of three students, who found that the (disembodied) embodied online activities outlined in Section 3 helped to inform their approaches to plays and performance texts:

> I love the creative learning... I feel like it is something which encourages you to think in a different way. It is so nice how on the module you can express yourself and develop your own opinions – you are never made to feel there is a right or wrong. Also these tasks are fun as well as useful – they don't

feel like work, but having completed them I always feel more confident about the text we are studying.

I have learned to focus on stage directions in a play just as much as the dialogue as sometimes when reading the stage directions we get more information and understand the play more.

I have learned the importance in considering the performative aspect of plays – bodies on stage, implicit directions, props etc. I would have deemed this less important than the text itself but I would definitely not do that anymore!

These three comments sum up what this Element has aimed to do. The activities on the previous pages offer ways to teach Shakespeare's plays *as drama*, within a Literature context: to help students to develop the ability to 'understand' the plays through their stage directions and cues for performance, both implicit and explicit, which are all too easily skimmed over on the page, but are fundamental to the plays' effects in performance. When we ask students to read plays, we ask them to engage with a conceptually complex idea: to read a text that is incomplete *as text*, that is at once a record of a past performance and a guide to a future performance, and that is shaped by assumptions about playing conditions that are invisible to us as a reader. Reading is always an act of time travel; reading a play involves looking to the past and the future at once. It also requires a doubled imagination: the reader must simultaneously conjure Weimann's *locus* and *platea*, both the imagined world of the play, and what Emma Smith has called the 'ludic theatre of the mind' (2008, p. 283). The aforementioned activities enable students to recognise, and to analyse, the 'performative aspects' of plays and performances by Shakespeare and his sisters, to understand the playing conditions that shaped these cues for performance, and to consider these elements as just as 'important' to their analysis as the texts themselves.

These activities also enable students to self-consciously involve their imaginations in the act of literary analysis. The student who commented 'I love the creative learning' mentions a number of pedagogical benefits: the opportunity to 'think in a different way'; to develop their 'own opinions'; to take pleasure in a learning process that is 'fun as well as useful'; and 'to feel more confident' about the texts that we are studying. This confidence is key; these pedagogical approaches enable students to become sources of authority by 'thinking in a different way', generating their own knowledge about and analysis of these texts through creative and embodied approaches.

The activities in this Element are only starting points. Activities 1 and 2 ask students to use their bodies to travel back in time; to consider embodiment, and its relationship to gender, status, and performance, in early modern England, through imaginatively embodying these states themselves. These experiences can inform a student's future work on any early modern playtext or performance text, in encouraging students to attend to gender, status, and the relationship between the playing space and the world of the play. Activities 2, 3, and 9 offer ways to close read Shakespearean plays through early modern performance conditions. Any early modern performance condition can be taught in this way: a single prop (a sword, a ring, the handkerchief in *Othello*); an architectural feature (the trapdoor, the balcony); boy actors' performances as female characters; make-up ('blackface' in the performance of blackness, and what Sujata Iyengar calls 'blushface' [2005, esp. pp. 123–39] in the performance of white femininity). Once a teacher has introduced a pertinent feature, and students have gained expertise in identifying performance cues through embodied activity, a student can be invited to close read an extract or scene in relation to that feature; or even, in a further example of peer-to-peer learning, to introduce this feature to their peers before sharing a brief close reading of its significance to a particular play. Activity 8 can enable students to explore these features in a contemporary production – or to explore how a contemporary 'original practices' production at Shakespeare's Globe or the American Shakespeare Center imagines such playing conditions from the past. Activity 7 uses characterisation as a way to explore the moral universe of an early modern play, the shifting sympathies and judgements of its characters, and how it might play on the sympathies and judgements of its audiences, in ways that can inform an argument about the play as a whole. Each of these activities, therefore, is designed to prepare students for more traditional, text-based literary work: seminar discussion, close readings, writing essays.

The Activities in Section 2 – 4, 5, and 6 – are distinct, but complementary, offering ways of recovering the performances, authorship, and voices of early modern women – and, through embodiment, ways of experiencing the works of these female theatre-makers as 'live'. These activities are offered as stand-alone in this section, but can of course be incorporated alongside Shakespeare-specific activities, enabling students to read across Shakespeare's plays and the theatre of his sisters. These too are starting points; once students have been introduced to the concept of 'performance texts', and the possibilities for female performance and storytelling in early modern England, students can be invited to find and present their own performance texts by Shakespeare's sisters. These might incorporate sources as diverse as a speech by Elizabeth I; a maidservant's deposition in a church court record; and a broadside ballad, written by a man but voicing a female character (and presumably available to be sung by a female singer, whether professional or amateur).[49] Students can therefore be invited to use the embodied activities in this section as a first step towards creating their own alternative canon – and to read Shakespeare's representations of women in conjunction with this canon, illuminating both sets of texts.

This Element, in the words of the final student quoted above, invites teachers of Shakespeare to 'consider' the 'importance' of 'bodies on stage'. The 'stage' here describes the professional playhouse stage where male bodies perform words by male authors, but also incorporates a wider range of bodies, stages, and voices: the (male and female) voices and bodies in masques, in household performances of closet drama, and in trials. This Element suggests that, in teaching Shakespeare's sisters alongside Shakespeare, and teaching both through embodiment and creativity, we can offer students the opportunity to read Shakespeare's plays as plays, within a rich theatrical world of male *and* female authorship and performance. In so doing, we can empower students to generate theatrically and historically informed readings of the plays of Shakespeare and his sisters through their bodies – and their imaginations.

---

[49] See Aughterson, 1995; Crawford and Gowing, 2000; Mansell and Hailwood; and Fumerton et al.

Bibliography

Primary Reading

Original primary sources are listed here, along with modern editions and anthologies; online archives can be found under 'Websites', below. All pre-1800 primary texts are listed with place and date of publication only.

Anon. (1592). *Arden of Faversham*, edited by Catherine Richardson (2022), London: Arden Early Modern Drama.

Anon. (1582). *A true and just Recorde, of the Information, Examination and Confession of All the Witches, taken at S. Oses in the countie of Essex*, London.

Anon. (1598). *The Apprehension and Confession of Three Notorious Witches*, London.

Aughterson, Kate, ed. (1995). *Renaissance Woman: A Sourcebook: Constructions of Femininity in England*, London: Routledge.

Cary, Elizabeth. (1613). *The Tragedy of Mariam*, edited by Ramona Wray (2012), London: Arden Early Modern Drama.

Cerasano, S. P., and Wynne-Davies, Marion, eds. (1996). *Renaissance Drama by Women: Texts and Documents*, London: Routledge.

Crawford, Patricia, and Gowing, Laura, eds. (2000). *Women's Worlds in Seventeenth-Century England: A Sourcebook*, London: Routledge.

Daniel, Samuel. (1601a). *An Edition of 'The Tragedie of Cleopatra' by Samuel Daniel*, edited by Dorothy Heather Bowles (2020). PhD Thesis: University of Sheffield, https://etheses.whiterose.ac.uk/28438/.

Daniel, Samuel. (1601b). *The Works of Samuel Daniel Newly Augmented*, London.

Daniel, Samuel. (1611a). *Certaine Small Workes Hertofore Divulged by Samuel Daniell*, London.

Daniel, Samuel. (1611b). *The Tragedie of Cleopatra*, London.

Dekker, Thomas, Ford, John, and Rowley, William. (1621a). *The Witch of Edmonton*, edited by Peter Corbin and Douglas Sedge (1997), Revels Student ed., Manchester: Manchester University Press.

Dekker, Thomas, Ford, John, and Rowley, William. (1621b). *The Witch of Edmonton*, edited by Lucy Munro (2017), London: Arden Early Modern Drama.

Fane, Rachel. (1627). 'Rachel Fane's *May Masque at Apethorpe*, 1627', edited by Marion O'Connor (2006), *English Literary Renaissance*, 36(1), 90–113.

Gibson, Marion, ed. (2000). *Early Modern Witches: Witchcraft Cases in Contemporary Writing*, London: Routledge.

Goodcole, Henry. (1621). *The Wonderfull Discoverie of Elizabeth Sawyer*, London.

Jones, Inigo. (1609a). 'House of Fame'. *Wikimedia*, https://commons .wikimedia.org/wiki/File:House_of_Fame_Jones.jpg.

Jones, Inigo. (1609b). 'Penthesilia'. *Wikimedia*, https://commons.wikime dia.org/wiki/File:Jones_Penthesilea.jpg.

Jonson, Ben. (1609). *Masque of Queens*, London.

Jonson, Ben. (1692). *Masque of Queens*. In Jonson's *Works*, edited by Clark J. Holloway (2002), http://hollowaypages.com/jonson1692fame.htm.

Peacham, Henry. (c.1594–5). 'Henry Peacham's Sketch of *Titus Andronicus*: Based on the Original in the Possession of the Marquis of Bath'. In 'A Performance of a Shakespeare Play', *Internet Shakespeare Editions*, University of Victoria, 28 September 2016, https://internetshakespeare .uvic.ca/Library/SLT/stage/staging/titus.html.

Pollard, Tanya, ed. (2004). *Shakespeare's Theater: A Sourcebook*, Oxford: Blackwell.

Purkiss, Diane, ed. (1998). *Three Tragedies by Renaissance Women*, London: Penguin.

Rosen, Barbara, ed. (1992). *Witchcraft in England, 1558–1618*, Amherst: University of Massachusetts Press.

Shakespeare, William. (1597). *Romeo and Juliet*, 2nd ed., edited by G. Blakemore Evans (2003), Cambridge: Cambridge University Press.

Shakespeare, William. (1603). *Hamlet*, 3rd ed., edited by Philip Edwards (2003), Cambridge: Cambridge University Press.

Shakespeare, William. (c.1606). *Macbeth*, 2nd ed., edited by A. R. Braunmuller (2008), Cambridge: Cambridge University Press.

Webster, John. (1612). *The White Devil*, edited by Benedict S. Robinson (2019), London: Arden Early Modern Drama.

Wroth, Mary. (c.1614–1619). *Love's Victory*, edited by Alison Findlay (2022), The Revels Plays, Manchester: Manchester University Press.

Secondary Reading

Abeysekera, Lakmal, and Dawson, Phillip. (2015). 'Motivation and the Cognitive Load in the Flipped Classroom: Definition, Rationale, and a Call for Research'. *Higher Education Research and Development* 34(1), 1–14.

Abrahamson, Dor, and Sánchez-García, Raul. (2016). 'Learning is Moving in New Ways: The Ecological Dynamics of Mathematics Education'. *Journal of the Learning Sciences* 25(2), 203–39.

Aebischer, Pascale, and Prince, Kathryn, eds. (2012). *Performing Early Modern Drama Today*, Cambridge: Cambridge University Press.

Angelo, Thomas A., and Cross, K. Patricia. (2013). *Classroom Assessment Techniques*, 2nd ed., New York: Jossey Bass.

Anon. (2016). 'Student Surveys are a Waste of Everyone's Time'. *Academics Anonymous* in *The Guardian*, 1 July, www.theguardian.com/

higher-education-network/2016/jul/01/student-surveys-are-a-waste-of-everyones-time.

Archer, Jayne Elisabeth, Goldring, Elizabeth, and Knight, Sarah, eds. (2007). *The Progresses, Pageants, and Entertainments of Queen Elizabeth I*, Oxford: Oxford University Press.

Arshad, Yasmin. (2019). *Imagining Cleopatra: Performing Gender and Power in Early Modern England*, London: Arden Shakespeare.

Arshad, Yasmin, Hackett, Helen, and Whipday, Emma. (2014). 'Daniel's *Cleopatra* and Lady Anne Clifford: From a Jacobean Portrait to Modern Performance'. *Early Theatre* 17(2), 167–86.

Awan, Omer A. (2021). 'Peer to Peer Learning: Its Importance and Benefits'. *Academic Radiology* 28(5), 747–8.

Bamford, Karen, and Leggatt, Alexander, eds. (2002). *Approaches to Teaching English Renaissance Drama*, New York: Modern Language Association of America.

Banks, Fiona. (2013). *Creative Shakespeare: The Globe Education Guide to Practical Shakespeare*, London: Arden Shakespeare.

Bargh, John A., and Schul, Yaacov. (1980). 'On the Cognitive Benefits of Teaching'. *Journal of Educational Psychology* 72(5), 593–604.

Barnett, Ronald, ed. (2005). *Reshaping the University: New Relationships between Research, Scholarship and Teaching*, Maidenhead: Open University Press.

Basit, Tehmina N., and Tomlinson, Sally, eds. (2012). *Social Inclusion and Higher Education*, Bristol: Bristol University Press, www.jstor.org/stable/j.ctt1t891n1.16.

Bendall, Sarah A. (2019). '"Take Measure of Your Wide and Flaunting Garments": The Farthingale, Gender and the Consumption of Space in Elizabethan and Jacobean England'. *Renaissance Studies* 33(5), 712–37.

Bertolet, Anna Riehl and Levin, Carole. (2018). *Creating the Premodern in the Postmodern Classroom: Creativity in Early English Literature and*

History Courses, Arizona Center for Medieval and Renaissance Studies, Chicago: University of Chicago Press.

Bevington, David. (2016). 'The Classroom'. In Dympna Callaghan and Suzanne Gossett, eds., *Shakespeare in Our Time: A Shakespeare Association of America Collection*, London: Arden Shakespeare, pp. 41–8.

Biet, Christian. (2011). 'Presence, Performance and Critical Pleasure: Play and Prerequisites in Research and Teaching'. In Derval Conroy and Danielle Clarke, eds., *Teaching the Early Modern Period*, Basingstoke: Palgrave Macmillan, pp. 263–9.

Biggs, John, and Tang, Catherine. (2007). *Teaching for Quality Learning at University: What the Student Does*, 3rd ed., Maidenhead: Open University Press.

Blackstone, Mary A. (2006). 'It's as if I'm Really Doing Research!'. In Elza C. Tiner, ed., *Teaching with the Records of Early English Drama*, Toronto: University of Toronto Press, pp. 27–47.

Blake, Felice. (2019). 'Why Black Lives Matter in the Humanities'. In Kimberlé Williams Crenshaw, Luke Charles Harris, Daniel Martinez HoSang, and George Lipsitz, eds., *Seeing Race Again: Countering Colorblindness across the Disciplines*, Oakland: University of California Press, pp. 307–26.

Bloom, Gina. (2012). '"My Feet See Better Than My Eyes": Spatial Mastery and the Game of Masculinity in *Arden of Faversham's* Amphitheatre'. *Theatre Survey* 53(1), 5–28.

Bonwell, Charles C., and Eison, James A. (1991). *Active Learning: Creating Excitement in the Classroom*, Washington, DC: Jossey-Bass.

Brannen, Anne. (2006). 'Using Historical Documents in the Literature Classroom: Elizabethan and Jacobean Court Cases'. In Elza C. Tiner, ed., *Teaching with the Records of Early English Drama*, Toronto: University of Toronto Press, pp. 87–96.

Bransford, John D., Brown, Ann L., and Cocking, Rodney R. (2000). *How People Learn: Brain, Mind, Experience, and School*, Washington, DC: National Academy Press.

Brook, Peter. (1968). *The Empty Space*, Penguin Modern Classics (2008), London: Penguin.

Brookfield, Stephen D. (1995). *Becoming a Critically Reflective Teacher*, San Francisco: Jossey-Bass.

Brookhart, Susan M. (2008). *How to Give Effective Feedback to Your Students*, Alexandria: Association for Supervision and Curriculum Development.

Brown, David Sterling. (2016). '(Early) Modern Literature: Crossing the Color-Line'. *Radical Teacher* (105), 69–77.

Burrows, Ian. (2020). *Shakespeare for Snowflakes: On Slapstick and Sympathy*, Winchester: Zero Books.

Callaghan, Dympna, and Gossett, Suzanne, eds. (2016). *Shakespeare in Our Time: A Shakespeare Association of America Collection*, London: Arden Shakespeare.

Callery, Dymphna. (2001). *Through the Body: A Practical Guide to Physical Theatre*, London: Nick Hern Books.

Carrington, Victoria, and Robinson, Muriel, eds. (2009). *Digital Literacies: Social Learning and Classroom Practices*, London: Sage.

Carson, Christie, and Kirwan, Peter, eds. (2014). *Shakespeare and the Digital World: Redefining Scholarship and Practice*, Cambridge: Cambridge University Press.

Cave, Richard. (2003). 'The Value of Practical Work and of Theatregoing in the Study of Seventeenth-Century Drama (1600–1640)'. *Literature Compass* 1, 1–12.

Chanock, Kate. (2000). 'Comments on Essays: Do Students Understand What Tutors Write?'. *Teaching in Higher Education* 5(1), 95–106.

Cohen, Ralph A. (1999). 'Original Staging and the Shakespeare Classroom'. In Milla Cozart Riggio, ed., *Teaching Shakespeare through Performance*, New York: Modern Language Association of America, pp. 78–101.

Cohen, Ralph A. (2018). *ShakesFear and How to Cure It: The Complete Handbook for Teaching Shakespeare*, London: Arden Shakespeare.

Conkie, Rob, and Maisano, Scott, eds. (2019). *Shakespeare and Creative Criticism*, New York: Berghahn.

Conroy, Derval, and Clarke, Danielle, eds. (2011). *Teaching the Early Modern Period*, Basingstoke: Palgrave Macmillan.

Corbett, Poppy, Kisby Compton, Anna, and Pooley, William G. (2022). *Creative Histories of Witchcraft: France, 1790–1940*, Cambridge: Cambridge University Press.

Cox Jensen, Freyja, and Whipday, Emma. (2017). '"Original Practices and Historical Imagination": Staging a Tragedie Called Merrie'. *Shakespeare Bulletin* 35(2), 289–307.

Cramp, Andy. (2012). 'Empowering "Non-traditional" Students in the UK: Feedback and the Hidden Curriculum'. In Tehmina N. Basit and Sally Tomlinson, eds., *Social Inclusion and Higher Education*, Bristol: Bristol University Press, pp. 237–254. www.jstor.org/stable/j.ctt1t891n1.16.

Crenshaw, Kimberlé Williams, Harris, Luke Charles, HoSang, Daniel Martinez, and Lipsitz, George, eds. (2019). *Seeing Race Again: Countering Colorblindness across the Disciplines*, Oakland: University of California Press.

Dadabhoy, Ambereen, and Mehdizadeh, Nedda. (2023). *Anti-Racist Shakespeare*, Cambridge Elements: Shakespeare and Pedagogy, Cambridge: Cambridge University Press.

Davidson, Peter, and Stevenson, Jane. (2007). 'Elizabeth I's Reception at Bisham (1592): Elite Women as Writers and Devisers'. In Jayne Elisabeth Archer, Elizabeth Goldring, and Sarah Knight, eds., *The* ography 85

Progresses, Pageants, and Entertainments of Queen Elizabeth I, Oxford: Oxford University Press, pp. 207–26.

Dessen, Alan C. (1999). 'Shakespeare's Theatrical Vocabulary and Today's Classroom'. In Milla Cozart Riggio, ed., *Teaching Shakespeare through Performance*, New York: Modern Language Association of America, pp. 63–77.

Donaweth, Jane. (1996). 'Teaching Shakespeare in the Context of Renaissance Women's Culture'. *Shakespeare Quarterly* 47(4), 476–89.

Dustagheer, Sarah, Jones, Oliver, and Rycroft, Eleanor. (2017). '(Re)constructed Spaces for Early Modern Drama: Research in Practice'. *Shakespeare Bulletin* 35(2), 173–85.

Dustagheer, Sarah, and Newman, Harry. (2018). 'Metatheatre and Early Modern Drama'. *Shakespeare Bulletin* 36(1), 3–18.

Dustagheer, Sarah, and Woods, Gillian, eds. (2017). *Stage Directions and Shakespearean Theatre*, London: Arden Shakespeare.

Edwards, Jennifer. (2020). '"Amorous Pinches": Keeping (In)tact in *Antony and Cleopatra*'. In Simon Smith, ed., *Shakespeare/Sense: Contemporary Readings in Sensory Culture*, London: Arden Shakespeare, pp. 157–77.

Eklund, Hillary, and Hyman, Wendy Beth, eds. (2019). *Teaching Social Justice through Shakespeare: Why Renaissance Literature Matters Now*, Edinburgh: Edinburgh University Press.

Erickson, Peter, and Hunt, Maurice, eds. (2005). *Approaches to Teaching Shakespeare's Othello*, New York: Modern Language Association of America.

Findlay, Alison. (2006). *Playing Spaces in Early Women's Drama*, Cambridge: Cambridge University Press.

Findlay, Alison. (2014). 'Reproducing *Iphigenia at Aulis*'. *Early Theatre* 17(2), 133–48.

Flaherty, Kate, Gay, Penny, and Semler, Liam E., eds. (2013). *Teaching Shakespeare Beyond the Centre*, Basingstoke: Palgrave Macmillan.

Fleming, Neil. (1992). 'Not Another Inventory, Rather a Catalyst for Reflection'. *To Improve the Academy* 11, 137–43, https://vark-learn.com/wp-content/uploads/2014/08/not_another_inventory.pdf.

Forward, Tony. (2005). *Shakespeare's Globe: An Interactive Pop-Up Theatre*, illustrated by Juan Wijngaard, London: Walker Books.

Frank, Arthur W. (2019). '"Who's There?": A Vulnerable Reading of *Hamlet*'. *Literature and Medicine* 37(2), 396–419.

Gibson, Marion. (2022). *The Witches of St Osyth*, Cambridge: Cambridge University Press.

Gibson, Rex. (1998). *Teaching Shakespeare: A Handbook for Teachers*, Cambridge School Shakespeare, Cambridge: Cambridge University Press.

Gikandi, Joyce W., and Morrow, Donna. (2016). 'Designing and Implementing Peer Formative Feedback within Online Learning Environments'. *Technology, Pedagogy and Education* 25(2), 153–70.

Gil Harris, Jonathan. (2007). 'The Smell of *Macbeth*'. *Shakespeare Quarterly* 58(4), 465–86.

Gilligan, Carol. (1991). 'Teaching Shakespeare's Sister: Notes from the Underground of Female Adolescence'. *Women's Studies Quarterly* 19(1), 31–51.

Gowing, Laura. (1996). *Domestic Dangers: Women, Words, and Sex in Early Modern London*, Oxford: Clarendon Press.

Gurr, Andrew. (2004). *Playgoing in Shakespeare's London*, 3rd ed., Cambridge: Cambridge University Press.

Gurr, Andrew, and Karim-Cooper, Farah, eds. (2014). *Moving Shakespeare Indoors: Performance and Repertoire in the Jacobean Playhouse*, Cambridge: Cambridge University Press.

Gutierrez, James. (2019). 'An Enactive Approach to Learning Music Theory? Obstacles and Openings'. *Frontiers in Education* 4, www.frontiersin.org/articles/10.3389/feduc.2019.00133/full.

Gutierrez, Nancy. (1996). 'Why William and Judith Both Need Their Own Rooms'. *Shakespeare Quarterly* 47(4), 424–32.

Hall, Kim F. (1996). 'Beauty and the Beast of Whiteness: Teaching Race and Gender'. *Shakespeare Quarterly* 47(4), 461–75.

Hara, Noriko. (2009). *Communities of Practice: Fostering Peer-to-Peer Learning and Informal Knowledge Sharing in the Work Place*, Bloomington: Springer.

Harwood, William S. (2000). 'The One-Minute Paper'. *Journal of Chemical Education* 73(3), 229–30.

Healey, Mick. (2005). 'Linking Research and Teaching Exploring Disciplinary Spaces and the Role of Inquiry-Based Learning'. In Ronald Barnett, ed., *Reshaping the University: New Relationships between Research, Scholarship and Teaching*, Maidenhead: Open University Press, pp. 67–78.

Hegland, Anna. (2021). 'Digital Innovation and Embodied Practice'. *Teaching Shakespeare* 21, 15–16.

Heron, Jonathan, Monk, Nicholas, and Prescott, Paul. (2012). 'Letting the Dead Come Out to Dance: An Embodied and Spatial Approach to Teaching Early Modern Drama'. In Pascale Aebischer and Kathryn Prince, eds., *Performing Early Modern Drama Today*, Cambridge: Cambridge University Press, pp. 162–77.

Hibbert, Paul. (2020). 'Reflective Frameworks for the Delivery of Teaching in Multiple Modes'. *MKE Paper Series* (BAM Management Knowledge and Education) 1, 1–16.

Hiscock, Andrew, and Hopkins, Lisa, eds. (2007). *Teaching Shakespeare and Early Modern Dramatists*, Basingstoke: Palgrave Macmillan.

Homan, Sidney, ed. (2019). *How and Why We Teach Shakespeare: College Teachers and Directors Share How They Explore the Playwright's Works with Their Students*, London: Routledge.

hooks, bell. (1994). *Teaching to Transgress: Education as the Practice of Freedom*, New York: Routledge.

Hurley, Ann. (2000). 'Archival Studies: Retrieving the "Nonexistent" Women Writers of the English Renaissance'. In Susanne Woods and Margaret P. Hannay, eds., *Teaching Tudor and Stuart Women Writers*, New York: Modern Language Association of America, pp. 252–7.

Iyengar, Sujata. (2005). *Shades of Difference: Mythologies of Skin Colour in Early Modern England*, Philadelphia: University of Pennsylvania Press.

Iyengar, Sujata. (2014). *Disability, Health, and Happiness in the Shakespearean Body*, New York: Routledge.

Jackson, Norman, Oliver, Martin, Shaw, Malcolm, and Wisdom, James, eds. (2006). *Developing Creativity in Higher Education: An Imaginative Curriculum*, London: Routledge.

Jackson, Philip W. (1968). *Life in Classrooms*, revised ed. (1990), New York: Teachers College Press.

Jacques, David. (1984). *Learning in Groups*, 3rd ed. (2000), London: Kogan Page.

Jowett, John. (2007). *Shakespeare and Text*, revised ed. (2019), Oxford: Oxford University Press.

Kamaralli, Anna. (2013). 'Teaching with Cue-scripts'. In Kate Flaherty, Penny Gay, and Liam E. Semler, eds., *Teaching Shakespeare Beyond the Centre*, Basingstoke: Palgrave Macmillan, pp. 169–79.

Karim-Cooper, Farah, and Stern, Tiffany, eds. (2015). *Shakespeare's Theatres and the Effects of Performance*, London: Arden Shakespeare.

Kember, David, and Ginns, Paul. (2012). *Evaluating Teaching and Learning: A Practical Handbook for Colleges, Universities and the Scholarship of Teaching*, London: Routledge.

Kember, David, and Kelly, Martin. (1993). *Improving Teaching through Action Research*, Campbelltown: Higher Education Research and Development Society of Australasia.

Kirwan, Peter. (2014a). '"From the Table of My Memory": Blogging Shakespeare In/Out of the Classroom'. In Christie Carson and Peter Kirwan, eds., *Shakespeare and the Digital World: Redefining Scholarship and Practice*, Cambridge: Cambridge University Press, pp. 100–12.

Kirwan, Peter. (2014b). 'Introduction to Part II: Defining Current Digital Scholarship and Practice: Shakespeare Pedagogy and the Digital Age'. In Christie Carson and Peter Kirwan, eds., *Shakespeare and the Digital World: Redefining Scholarship and Practice*, Cambridge: Cambridge University Press, pp. 58–62.

Knutson, Roslyn L., McInnis, David, and Steggle, Matthew, eds. (2020). *Loss and the Literary Culture of Shakespeare's Time*, Basingstoke: Palgrave Macmillan.

Korda, Natasha. (2011). *Labors Lost: Women's Work and the Early Modern Stage*, Philadelphia: University of Pennsylvania Press.

Kumpulainen, Kristiina, and Wray, David. (2002). *Classroom Interaction and Social Learning: From Theory to Practice*, New York: Routledge.

Lave, Jean, and Wenger, Etiene. (1991). *Situated Learning: Legitimate Peripheral Participation*, Cambridge: Cambridge University Press.

Leathwood,Carole, and O'Connell, Paul. (2003). '"It's a Struggle": The Construction of the "New Student" in Higher Education'. *Journal of Education Policy* 18, 597–615.

Leggatt, Alexander, and Bamford, Karen, eds. (2002). *Approaches to Teaching Renaissance Drama*, New York: Modern Language Association of America.

Lengel, Traci, and Kuczala, Mike. (2010). *The Kinesthetic Classroom: Teaching and Learning through Movement*, Thousand Oaks: Sage.

Lewis, Sarah, and Whipday, Emma. (2019). 'Sounding Offstage Worlds: Experiencing Liminal Space and Time in *Macbeth* and *Othello*'. *Shakespeare* 15(3), 272–82.

Loftis, Sonya Freeman. (2021). *Shakespeare and Disability Studies*, Oxford: Oxford University Press.

Maguire, Laurie. (2002). 'Teaching Cary's *The Tragedy of Mariam* through Performance'. In Alexander Leggatt and Karen Bamford, eds., *Approaches to Teaching Renaissance Drama*, New York: Modern Language Association of America, pp. 95–8.

Maguire, Laurie, ed. (2008). *How to Do Things with Shakespeare: New Approaches, New Essays*, Oxford: Blackwell.

May, Steven W. (2021). 'The Renaissance Women's Canon, Past, Present, and Future'. *Criticism* 63(1–2), 131–40.

McDonald, Russ. (2009). 'Planned Obsolescence or Working at the Words'. In G. B. Shand, ed., *Teaching Shakespeare: Passing It On*, Oxford: Blackwell, pp. 27–42.

McManus, Clare. (2002). *Women on the Renaissance Stage: Anna of Denmark and Female Masquing at the Stuart Court (1590–1619)*, Manchester: Manchester University Press.

McManus, Clare. (2008). 'When Is a Woman Not a Woman? Or, Jacobean Fantasies of Female Performance (1606–1611)'. *Modern Philology* 105(3), 437–74.

Monk, Nicholas, Chillington Rutter, Carol, Neelands, Jonothan, and Heron, Jonathan. (2011). *Open-Space Learning: A Study in Transdisciplinary Pedagogy*, London: Bloomsbury Academic.

Morss, Kate, and Murray, Rowena. (2005). *Teaching at University: A Guide for Postgraduates and Researchers*, London: Sage.

Munro, Lucy, and Whipday, Emma. (2020). 'Making Early Modern "Verbatim Theater," or, "Keep the Widow Waking"'. In Roslyn L. Knutson, David McInnis, and Matthew Steggle, eds., *Loss and the Literary Culture of Shakespeare's Time*, Basingstoke: Palgrave Macmillan, pp. 233–349.

Ostovich, Helen. (2007). 'Early Modern Theatre History'. In Andrew Hiscock and Lisa Hopkins, eds., *Teaching Shakespeare and Early Modern Dramatists*, Basingstoke: Palgrave Macmillan, pp. 14–45.

Palfrey, Simon. (2011). *Doing Shakespeare*, London: Arden Shakespeare.

Panjwani, Varsha. (2022). *Podcasts and Feminist Shakespeare Pedagogy*, Cambridge Elements: Shakespeare and Pedagogy, Cambridge: Cambridge University Press.

Perritt Lee, Elizabeth. (1997). 'The Learning Response Log: An Assessment Tool'. *The English Journal* 86(1), 41–4.

Purcell, Stephen. (2017). 'Practice-as-Research and Original Practices'. *Shakespeare Bulletin* 35(3), 425–43.

Purkiss, Diane. (1996). *The Witch in History*, London: Routledge.

Raber, Karen. (2007). 'Early Modern Women Dramatists'. In Andrew Hiscock and Lisa Hopkins, eds., *Teaching Shakespeare and Early Modern Dramatists*, Basingstoke: Palgrave Macmillan, pp. 218–34.

Rackin, Phyllis. (2016). 'Why Feminism Still Matters'. In Dympna Callaghan and Suzanne Gossett, eds., *Shakespeare in Our Time: A Shakespeare Association of America Collection*, London: Arden Shakespeare, pp. 7–13.

Ramsden, Paul. (1992). *Learning to Teach in Higher Education*, London: Routledge.

Richards, Jennifer. (2019). *Voices and Books in the English Renaissance: A New History of Reading*, Oxford: Oxford University Press.

Riggio, Milla Cozart, ed. (1999). *Teaching Shakespeare through Performance*, New York: Modern Language Association of America.

Rocklin, Edward L. (2005). *Performance Approaches to Teaching Shakespeare*, Urbana: National Council of Teachers of English.

Rowley, Jennifer. (2003). 'Designing Student Feedback Questionnaires'. *Quality Assurance in Education* 11(3), 142–9.

Shand, G. B., ed. (2009). *Teaching Shakespeare: Passing It On*, Oxford: Blackwell.

Smith, Bruce. (1999). *The Acoustic World of Early Modern England*, Chicago: Chicago University Press.

Smith, Emma. (2008). '"Freezing the Snowman": (How) Can We Do Performance Criticism?'. In Laurie Maguire, ed. *How to Do Things with Shakespeare: New Approaches, New Essays*, Oxford: Blackwell, pp. 280–97.

Smith, Simon. (2017). *Musical Response in the Early Modern Playhouse, 1603–1625*, Cambridge: Cambridge University Press.

Smith, Simon, ed. (2020). *Shakespeare/Sense: Contemporary Readings in Sensory Culture*, London: Arden Shakespeare.

Smith, Simon, and Whipday, Emma, eds. (2022). *Playing and Playgoing in Early Modern England: Actor, Audience and Performance*, Cambridge: Cambridge University Press.

Sousa, David A. (2011). *How the Brain Learns*, 4th ed., Thousand Oaks: Corwin Press.

Stern, Tiffany. (2004). *Making Shakespeare: From Stage to Page*, London: Routledge.

Stern, Tiffany. (2015). '"This Wide and Universal Theatre": The Theatre as Prop in Shakespeare's Metadrama'. In Farah Karim-Cooper and Tiffany Stern, eds. *Shakespeare's Theatres and the Effects of Performance*, London: Arden Shakespeare, pp. 11–32.

Stern, Tiffany, ed. (2020). *Rethinking Theatrical Documents in Shakespeare's England*, London: Arden Shakespeare.

Strayer, Jeremy F. (2012). 'How Learning in an Inverted Classroom Influences Cooperation, Innovation and Task Orientation'. *Learning Environments Research* 15(2), 171–93.

Straznicky, Marta. (2004). *Privacy, Playreading, and Women's Closet Drama, 1550–1700*, Cambridge: Cambridge University Press.

Sullivan, Erin. (2014). 'Internal and External Shakespeare: Constructing the Twenty-First-Century Classroom'. In Christie Carson and Peter Kirwan, eds., *Shakespeare and the Digital World: Redefining Scholarship and Practice*, Cambridge: Cambridge University Press, pp. 63–74.

Swale, Jessica. (2015). *Drama Games for Classrooms and Workshops*, London: Nick Hern Books.

Thew, Neil. (2006). 'Teaching Shakespeare: A Survey of the Undergraduate Level in Higher Education'. *HEA English Subject Centre Report Series* 13, 1–33.

Thomas, Miranda Fay. (2019). '"And So Everyone According to His Cue": Practice-led Teaching and Cue-scripts in the Classroom'. In Sidney Homan, ed. *How and Why We Teach Shakespeare: College Teachers and Directors Share How They Explore the Playwright's Works with Their Students*, London: Routledge, pp. 128–37.

Thompson, Ayanna, and Turchi, Laura. (2016). *Teaching Shakespeare with Purpose: A Student-Centered Approach*, London: Bloomsbury.

Tiner, Elza C., ed. (2006). *Teaching with the Records of Early English Drama*, Toronto: University of Toronto Press.

Tullis, Jonathan G., and Goldstone, Robert L. (2020). 'Why Does Peer Instruction Benefit Student Learning?'. *Cognitive Research* 5(15), https://doi.org/10.1186/s41235-020-00218-5.

Wagner Cook, Susan, Mitchell, Zachary, and Goldin-Meadow, Susan. (2008). 'Gesturing Makes Learning Last'. *Cognition* 106(2), 1047–58.

Wall, Wendy. (2016). 'Letters, Characters, Roots'. In Dympna Callaghan and Suzanne Gossett, eds., *Shakespeare in Our Time: A Shakespeare Association of America Collection*, London: Arden Shakespeare, pp. 18–22.

Weimann, Robert. (2000). *Author's Pen and Actor's Voice: Playing and Writing in Shakespeare's Theatre*, edited by Helen Higbee and William West, Cambridge: Cambridge University Press.

Wenger, Etienne. (1991). *Communities of Practice: Learning, Meaning and Identity*, Cambridge: Cambridge University Press.

Whipday, Emma. (2019a). *Shakespeare's Domestic Tragedies: Violence in the Early Modern Home*, Cambridge: Cambridge University Press.

Whitfield, Petronella. (2020). *Teaching Strategies for Neurodiversity and Dyslexia in Actor Training: Sensing Shakespeare*, London: Routledge.

Williams, Nora J. (2019). 'Writing the Collaborative Process: *Measure (Still) for Measure*, Shakespeare, and Rape Culture'. *PARtake: The Journal of Performance as Research* 2(1), https://partakejournal.org/index.php/partake/article/view/401/383.

Winston, Joe. (2015). *Transforming the Teaching of Shakespeare with the Royal Shakespeare Company*, London: Arden Shakespeare.

Woods, Gillian. (2017). 'Understanding Dumb Shows and Interpreting *The White Devil*'. In Sarah Dustagheer and Gillian Woods, eds. *Stage Directions and Shakespearean Theatre*, London: Arden Shakespeare, pp. 287–310.

Woods, Susanne, and Hannay, Margaret P., eds. (2000). *Teaching Tudor and Stuart Women Writers*, New York: Modern Language Association of America.

Unpublished Theses

Coker, Helen. (2017). 'Understanding Pedagogic Collaboration in the Online Environment'. PhD Thesis: University of Edinburgh.

Folley, Susan. (2013). 'Bridging the Gap between Face-to-Face and Online Teaching: A Case Study Exploring Tutors' Early Experiences of

Teaching Online in a UK University 2009–2012'. PhD Thesis: University of Huddersfield.

Performances

Cary, Elizabeth. (1995). *The Tragedy of Mariam*. Directed by Elizabeth Schafer and recorded in October, Royal Holloway, www.youtube.com/watch?v=TOYsjNcG93w.

Daniel, Samuel. (2013). *The Tragedie of Cleopatra*. Directed by Emma Whipday, produced by Yasmin Arshad, and executive produced by Helen Hackett, performed at Goodenough College for UCL on 3 March, https://vimeo.com/302836585.

Jonson, Ben. (2016). *Masque of Queens*. Directed by Emma Whipday and produced by Nadine Akkerman and Daniel Starza Smith, New College Chapel, Oxford, 11 August for Shakespeare400, King's College London, https://shakespeare400.kcl.ac.uk/kings-blog/ben-jonsons-masque-queens/.

Lumley, Lady Jane. (2013). *Iphigenia at Aulis*. Directed by Emma Rucastle for The Rose Company, 24 November, UCL (on tour).

Lumley, Lady Jane. (2020). *Iphigeneya*. Directed by Tom Bishop and introduced by Deanne Williams, at 'The Female Experience in Early Modern England' symposium, University of Auckland, 7 November, www.youtube.com/watch?v=MMIl71x_l2M.

Shakespeare, William. (2013). *Twelfth Night* (clip), Shakespeare's Globe, *Opus Arte*, recorded in June 2012, www.youtube.com/watch?v=RDPT2e26SgY.

Websites

Arizona Center for Medieval and Renaissance Studies. (2021). 'Education: A RaceB4Race Symposium', https://acmrs.asu.edu/RaceB4Race/Education.

A Bit Lit. (2020a). 'Stay at Home Shakespeare 1: Emma Whipday Talks Witchcraft, Magic and Murder in *Macbeth*'. 2 April, https://abitlit.co/schools/stay-at-home-shakespeare-1-emma-whipday-talks-witchcraft-magic-and-murder-in-macbeth/.

A Bit Lit. (2020b). 'Stay at Home Shakespeare 2: Emma Whipday on the Balcony in *Romeo and Juliet*'. 9 April, https://abitlit.co/series/stay-at-home-shakespeare-2-emma-whipday-on-the-balcony-in-romeo-and-juliet/.

A Bit Lit. (2021). 'Engendering the Stage: Making Space for an Inclusive Performance History'. 24 November, https://abitlit.co/history/engendering-the-stage-making-space-for-an-inclusive-performance-history/.

Bochicchio, Sarah. (2020). '1500–1599'. *Fashion History Timeline*, State University of New York, 18 August, https://fashionhistory.fitnyc.edu/1590-1599/.

Box of Broadcasts (BoB), https://learningonscreen.ac.uk/ondemand/.

The British Library. (1609). 'Autograph Manuscript of Ben Jonson's *The Masque of Queens*, 1609'. *Discovering Literature*, www.bl.uk/collection-items/autograph-manuscript-of-ben-jonsons-the-masque-of-queens-1609.

The British Library. 'Elizabethan Dress Codes'. *Learning*, www.bl.uk/learning/timeline/item126628.html.

Cockett, Peter, Gough, Melinda, Munro, Lucy, and McManus, Clare. (n. d.). *Engendering the Stage*, https://engenderingthestage.humanities.mcmaster.ca/.

Compton, Lindsey. (2020). 'Lecture Watch Parties: Creating Community and Maximising Learning Opportunity- MicroCPD'. *HEFi News and*

Media, University of Birmingham, 30 November, www.birmingham.ac
.uk/university/hefi/news/2020/12/lecture-watch-parties-creating-
community-and-maximising-learning-opportunity-microcpd.aspx.

Dadabhoy, Ambereen. (2021). 'All Our Othellos: Reading Race through
Teaching Editions of the Play'. *RaceB4Race Symposium on Education*,
22 January, www.youtube.com/watch?v=rBiWdcshiaU&t=7s.

Dadabhoy, Ambereen, and Mehdizadeh, Nedda. (2020). 'Cultivating an Anti-
Racist Pedagogy'. *Folder Shakespeare Library: Critical Race Conversations*,
https://www.youtube.com/watch?v=_4oCWstlcPc.

Drama Online, https://dramaonlinelibrary.com/.

Essex Witch Trials, www.witchtrials.co.uk.

Folger Shakespeare Library. (2020). ' Critical Race Conversations'. 9 July,
www.youtube.com/watch?v=_4oCWstlcPc.

Folger Shakespeare Library. *Early Modern Manuscripts Online*, https://
emmo.folger.edu/.

Folger Shakespeare Library. 'The Folger Method'. *Teach and Learn*, www
.folger.edu/the-folger-method.

Fumerton, Patricia et al. *Early Broadside Ballads Archive*, University of
California at Santa Barbara, Department of English, https://ebba.english
.ucsb.edu/.

MacNeill, Fiona. (2021). 'Watch Parties: What, Why, Who, Where,
How?'. Elearning Team, University of Brighton, 3 March, https://
blogs.brighton.ac.uk/elearningteam/2021/03/03/watch-parties-what-
why-who-where-how/.

Mansell, Charmian, and Hailwood, Mark, eds. (n.d.). *Court Depositions of
South-West England, 1500–1700*, University of Exeter, http://huma
nities-research.exeter.ac.uk/womenswork/courtdepositions/.

MIT. *Global Shakespeares Video and Performance Archive*, https://global
shakespeares.mit.edu/.

Myles, Robert. *The Show Must Go Online*, https://robmyles.co.uk/the showmustgoonline/.

The National Archives. 'Early Modern Witch Trials'. *Classroom Resources*, www.nationalarchives.gov.uk/education/resources/early-modern-witch-trials/.

Ortelia Interactive Spaces. (2012). 'The Rose Theatre Virtual Environment'. 9 May, www.youtube.com/watch?v=EApTZ1QuoHs&list=UU_NPXATOchnA2Q0QU6jZtmA&index=41.

Padlet, https://en-gb.padlet.com/.

Ray, Benjamin. *Salem Witch Trials Documentary Archive and Transcription Project*, University of Virginia, https://salem.lib.virginia.edu/home.html.

Reddit. 'Am I the Asshole', www.reddit.com/r/AmItheAsshole/.

The Rose Company, https://therosecompany.posthaven.com/.

Sander, Libby, and Bauman, Oliver. (2020). 'Zoom Fatigue is Real: Here's Why Video Calls are so Draining'. *TED Ideas*, 19 May, https://ideas.ted.com/zoom-fatigue-is-real-heres-why-video-calls-are-so-draining/.

Shakespeare Association of America. (2014). 'Resurrecting Shakespeare (and His Sisters)'. SAA Annual Meeting, St Louis, www.shakespeareassociation.org/wp-content/uploads/2018/04/Resurrecting-Shakespeare-correspondence-.pdf.

Shakespeare Birthplace Trust. 'Shakespeare's Theatres', www.shakespeare.org.uk/education/teaching-resources/shakespeares-theatre/.

Shakespearean London Theatres. De Montfort University, V&A, and AHRC, http://shalt.dmu.ac.uk/index.html.

Shakespeare's Globe. *Globe Player*, www.shakespearesglobe.com/watch/.

Shakespeare's Globe. *Virtual Tour*, www.shakespearesglobe.com/discover/about-us/virtual-tour/.

Starza Smith, Daniel. (2016). 'Ben Jonson's *Masque of Queens'*. *Shakespeare400*, King's College London, 11 August, https://shake speare400.kcl.ac.uk/kings-blog/ben-jonsons-masque-queens/.

The Tudor Tailor. (2020–1). 'Who Do You Think You Were?', www .youtube.com/c/TheTudorTailor.

University of Auckland. (2020). 'The Female Experience in Early Modern England'. 6 November, www.youtube.com/watch? v=MMIl71x_l2M.

Wall, John et al. *Virtual Pauls' Cross Project: A Digital Re-creation of John Donne's Gunpowder Day sermon, London 1622*, https://vpcp.chass.ncsu .edu/.

Wall, Wendy, Knight, Leah. (2021). 'Teaching with the Pulter Project Symposium'. 30 April–7 May, www.youtube.com/watch?v=uz7ED GbmT8Y.

Whipday, Emma. (2019b). 'Witches at Night: Creative Responses to Early Modern Witch Trials'. *Inner Lives: Emotions, Identity, and the Supernatural, 1300–1900*, 16 September, https://innerlives.org/2019/09/16/witches-at-night-creative-responses-to-early-modern-witch-trials/.

Zafar-Arif, Shehrazade. (2016). 'How Have Performances of Shakespeare Changed Over Time'. *British Council Voices Magazine*, 6 April, www .britishcouncil.org/voices-magazine/how-have-performances-shake speare-changed-over-time.

Icon Credit

Icon images used in the Activity boxes are from lushik/DigitalVision Vectors/Getty Images.

Cambridge Elements ≡

Shakespeare and Pedagogy

Liam E. Semler
University of Sydney

Liam E. Semler is Professor of Early Modern Literature in the Department of English at the University of Sydney. He is author of *Teaching Shakespeare and Marlowe: Learning versus the System* (2013) and co-editor (with Kate Flaherty and Penny Gay) of *Teaching Shakespeare beyond the Centre: Australasian Perspectives* (2013). He is editor of *Coriolanus: A Critical Reader* (2021) and co-editor (with Claire Hansen and Jackie Manuel) of *Reimagining Shakespeare Education: Teaching and Learning through Collaboration* (Cambridge, forthcoming). His most recent book outside Shakespeare studies is *The Early Modern Grotesque: English Sources and Documents 1500–1700* (2019). Liam leads the Better Strangers project which hosts the open-access Shakespeare Reloaded website (shakespearereloaded.edu.au).

Gillian Woods
Birkbeck College, University of London

Gillian Woods is Reader in Renaissance Literature and Theatre at Birkbeck College, University of London. She is the author of *Shakespeare's Unreformed Fictions* (2013; joint winner of Shakespeare's Globe Book Award), *Romeo and Juliet: A Reader's Guide to Essential Criticism* (2012), and numerous articles about Renaissance drama. She is the co-editor (with Sarah Dustagheer) of *Stage Directions and Shakespearean Theatre* (2018). She is currently working on a new edition of *A Midsummer Night's Dream* for Cambridge University Press, as well as a Leverhulme-funded monograph about *Renaissance Theatricalities*.

As founding director of the Shakespeare Teachers' Conversations, she runs a seminar series that brings together university academics, school teachers, and educationalists from non-traditional sectors, and she regularly runs workshops for schools.

About the Series

The teaching and learning of Shakespeare around the world is complex and changing. *Elements in Shakespeare and Pedagogy* synthesises theory and practice, including provocative, original pieces of research, as well as dynamic, practical engagements with learning contexts.

Cambridge Elements ☰

Shakespeare and Pedagogy

Printed in the United States
by Baker & Taylor Publisher Services